· **BARBARA KINGSOLVER'S**

The
Poisonwood
Bible

A READER'S GUIDE

LINDA WAGNER-MARTIN

CONTINUUM | NEW YORK | LONDON

2001

The Continuum International Publishing Group Inc
370 Lexington Avenue, New York, NY 10017

The Continuum International Publishing Group Ltd
The Tower Building, 11 York Road, London SE1 7NX

Printed in the United States of America

Library of Congress Cataloging-in-Publication Data

Wagner-Martin, Linda.
    Barbara Kingsolver's The poisonwood Bible / Linda Wagner-Martin.
        p. cm. — (Continuum contemporaries)
    Includes bibliographical references.
    ISBN 0-8264-5234-5 (alk. paper)
    1. Kingsolver, Barbara. Poisonwood Bible.   2. Congo (Democratic
Republic) — In literature.   3. Missionaries in literature.   I. Title.
II. Series.
    PS3561.I496 P65 2001
    813'.54 — dc21

                                                      2001028738

Barbara Kingsolver's
The Poisonwood Bible

Also available in this series

Pat Barker's *Regeneration*, by Karin Westman
Kazuo Ishiguro's *The Remains of the Day*, by Adam Parkes
Carol Shields's *The Stone Diaries*, by Abby Werlock
J.K. Rowling's *Harry Potter Novels*, by Philip Nel
Jane Smiley's *A Thousand Acres*, by Susan Farrell
Louis De Bernieres's *Captain Corelli's Mandolin*, by Con Coroneos
Irvine Welsh's *Trainspotting*, by Robert Morace
Toni Morrison's *Paradise*, by Kelly Reames
Donna Tartt's *The Secret History*, by Tracy Hargreaves

Forthcoming in this series

Kate Atkinson's *Behind the Scenes at the Museum*, by Emma Parker
Haruki Murakami's *The Wind-up Bird Chronicle*, by Matthew Strecher
Jonathan Coe's *What a Carve Up!*, by Pamela Thurschwell
Don DeLillo's *Underworld*, by John Duvall
Annie Proulx's *The Shipping News*, by Aliki Varvogli
Graham Swift's *Last Orders*, by Pamela Cooper
Michael Ondaatje's *The English Patient*, by John Bolland
Ian Rankin's *Black and Blue*, by Gill Plain
Bret Easton Ellis's *American Psycho*, by Julian Murphet
Cormac McCarthy's *All the Pretty Horses*, by Stephen Tatum
Iain Banks's *Complicity*, by Cairns Craig
A.S. Byatt's *Possession*, by Catherine Burgass
David Guterson's *Snow Falling on Cedars*, by Jennifer Haytock
Helen Fielding's *Bridget Jones's Diary*, by Imelda Whelehan
Sebastian Faulks's *Birdsong*, by Pat Wheeler
Hanif Kureishi's *The Buddha of Suburbia*, by Nahem Yousaf
Nick Hornby's *High Fidelity*, by Joanne Knowles
Zadie Smith's *White Teeth*, by Claire Squires
Arundhati Roy's *The God of Small Things*, by Julie Mullaney
Alan Warner's *Morvern Callar*, by Sophy Dale
Vikram Seth's *A Suitable Boy*, by Angela Atkins
Margaret Atwood's *Alias Grace*, by Gina Wisker

Contents

1.
The Novelist   7

2.
The Novel   20

3.
The Novel's Reception 56

4.
The Novel's Performance   65

5.
Further Reading and Discussion Questions   71

Notes   77

Bibliography   83

The Novelist

The time was a warm Saturday afternoon, October 28, 2000. The place was the expanded and remodeled barn which the bookstore in the small North Carolina village used for important writer's appearances. On this day, the barn was filled to capacity—and beyond—by the eager readers who had bought all of the 600 tickets available the first day they went on sale. The speaker was the tall, kindly-looking Barbara Kingsolver, on tour to read from her just-published novel, *Prodigal Summer*, the first of her novels to be set in the location of her birth, the South, a country of modest lives and equally modest fortunes.

One of her opening anecdotes, in fact, was chosen to make the point that she was Southern eminently clear. Looking intently at her audience, Kingsolver smiled and apologized for the fact that there had been tickets sold for her reading. Her dilemma as a writer, she explained to the sympathetic audience (already won over by her natural manner and lower register voice), stemmed from her having been born and raised in Kentucky. Trained to be a modest, soft-spoken Southern girl, Kingsolver found traveling from city to city—giving readings and interviews but above all selling and signing books—the epitome of behavior Southern women should avoid at any cost. Whenever she published a new book, she was tortured by this contradiction between who Barbara Kingsolver really was (the modest writer of Southern descent) and the role she felt compelled—by her agent and her publishers—to play as author.

The solution to the problem, she continued, had this time been inherent in the novel itself. Because *Prodigal Summer* was about ecological efforts, focusing on the various misuses of chemicals and other harmful practices now rampant in the civilized world, Kingsolver would give the proceeds from each of her appearances to support the work of a local or area ecological group. The author tour would thereby become more than an individual ego trip.

It is this sense of Kingsolver as real person, with commitments and beliefs she adheres to regardless of their popularity, that wins her readers. The sense of identity does not, however, carry over to these readers' appreciation of her fiction: Kingsolver is not an autobiographical writer. Or she is not exclusively an autobiographical writer. She instead finds experiences, characters, and events, that are germane to the experiences of her many readers: she seems to know how readers hunger for a sense of reality, particularly the reality of women's life experiences. If *The Poisonwood Bible* is the most exotic of her novels, placing her finely drawn characters for the most part in the context of 1960s Congolese Africa, her other works—*The Bean Trees, Pigs in Heaven*, the stories and essays, and *Animal Dreams*—create moving narratives out of events, and locations, that are all too commonplace.

The words *modest* and *Southern* recur when one thinks of Barbara Kingsolver. Born April 8, 1955, in Maryland, she grew up in rural eastern Kentucky (Nicholas County), an integral part of the very small Appalachian community. Her father, the area's doctor, and her mother, a well educated woman, wanted Barbara and her sister and brother to have the normal experiences of living simply in the naturally beautiful country. Aside from farming and raising tobacco, the chief industry of the region was coal mining: the people Kingsolver grew up among were working class, a description that translates economically to lower middle class and, sometimes, middle class. There were few chances to dream grandly; most of the town's children either did the same work their parents had done, or left the area to find work elsewhere. Few went to college. Barbara and her siblings, having more intellectual resources than most of their classmates, were outsiders to the mainstream culture.[1]

Kingsolver's mother, Virginia Lee Henry, combined her love of gardening and bird watching with her community activism. Born in Lexington, Kentucky, she enjoyed living near her parents, being a good helpmeet to—and partner in—her husband's life as the town's physician. In Kingsolver's 1997 essay about her mother, she recounts this story:

I am sitting on your lap and you are crying. *Thank you honey, thank you so much,* you say over and over, rocking back and forth as you hold me in the straight-backed kitchen chair. I've brought you flowers—the sweet peas you must have spent all spring trying to grow, training them up the trellis in the yard. You had nothing to work with but weeks of gray rain and the patience of a young wife at home with pots and pans and small children trying to create just one beautiful thing, something to take you outside our little white clapboard house on East Main. I never noticed until all at once they burst through the trellis in a pink red purple dazzle. A finger painting of colors humming against the blue air: I could think of nothing but to bring it to you. I climbed up the wooden trellis and picked the flowers. Every one.[2]

What remains of the child's memory is the mother's sweetness. She does not criticize or lament. She thanks. Kingsolver also describes the joy she felt learning about the natural world beside her mother: "When I close my eyes I discover it's there, an endless field of flowers. Columbines, blue asters, daisies, sweet peas, zinnias. One single flower bed stretching out for miles in every direction. I am small enough to watch the butterflies come. I know them from the pasture behind our house, butterflies you taught me to love and name: monarchs, Dianas, tiger swallowtails. I follow their lazy zig-zag as they visit every flower. . . . We stay there in the dark for a long time, you and I, both of us with our eyes closed watching the butterflies drift so slowly, filling up as much time as forever."[3]

All the Kingsolvers were readers, and read books more often than they watched television. While Barbara Kingsolver majored in subjects other than English in college and graduate school, she had the sense of the importance, and love, of language early on: it never left her. She knew she was a person of words, and a possible writer, from her childhood.

Her father, who had come from a very poor Kentucky family and put himself through medical school, abhorred television, so when the family's set broke, it was twelve years before he had it repaired.[4] His grandmother was Cherokee, and while he did not prevent his wife and children from practicing their protestant religion, his own belief system may have been closer to a Native American spirituality. As Kingsolver recalls about her father, "His idea of worship is to sit in a forest and listen to the birds. . . . he was always driven to serve people who needed him, whether they could pay or not. When I was in grade school [8 or 9 months of her second grade year, 1963] we lived in Africa and in the Caribbean for a while. We didn't have very much. In Africa we didn't have running water. . . ."[5] Kingsolver said subsequently that the experience of living in Africa "as a minority" changed her life.[6]

She describes her adolescence as stormy, her close ties with her mother somewhat painful at that time. She needed to go away for her college experiences, and she did so, attending DePauw University in Indiana on a music scholarship. "Radical" in her anti-war protests, tough in her militaristic dress, Kingsolver looked anything but the modest Southerner in those years of the mid 1970s. Ashamed of what her college classmates called her "accent," she taught herself to speak without any hint of her Kentucky lineage. She was her own butterfly, leaving behind in Kentucky the cocoon of her childhood and adolescence. She protested Vietnam involvement, lived and ran with the aggressively liberal group on campus, and went home only as often as she had to.

Kingsolver's fascination with observing life, and trying to find strands of meaning and patterns in her observations, led her to major in ecology and evolutionary biology. She explored all facets of knowledge — science, yes, but also political philosophy (especially Marx and Engels) and feminist thought. Throughout the four years, in her words, she "wrote furtively in my little notebooks."[7] She lived as an "independent"; she dated; and she was raped — by an acquaintance.[8] (In the mid-1970s, there was no recourse against "date rape": she suffered in shamed silence; her attacker was never punished.)

Graduating from DePauw in 1977, Kingsolver found ways to live in Europe for several years. She would not be one of those Carlisle, Kentucky natives who went home to live: the world was too exciting, and she had ample skills to support herself. In France and Greece she worked as a copy editor, housecleaner, X-ray technician, archaeologist, biological researcher and translator of medical documents. (One reason for her years abroad was to learn to speak other languages; another was her search "for a way to be in the world.")[9]

When she returned to the States and began graduate study in the early 1980s, she saw her study at the University of Arizona as further exploration. Along with her conventional courses, she took a fiction writing class (only the second writing course in her experience; she had taken one at DePauw) from the novelist Francine Prose.

Prose not only encouraged her but, perhaps more important, gave her a book of Kentucky writer Bobbie Ann Mason's to read. After decades of reading Doris Lessing, Eudora Welty, and Flannery O'Connor, Kingsolver in Mason found a voice more contemporary with her own time and life: she understood that she could become a writer.

In the midst of her doctoral dissertation, Kingsolver accepted a scientific writing job at the University of Arizona, telling her dissertation committee she needed a year off to think over career options. She then took the M.A. degree, married a scientist, and began her free-lance writing career, all the while writing scientific articles, grant proposals, reports (on algae in sewage systems), and the kinds of technical writing projects she was hired to produce.

She wrote poems. She wrote stories. She wrote newspaper articles, and through her interest in becoming an Arizona journalist, she began sustained coverage of the Phelps Dodge Copper mine strike in 1983 (the strike would last for eighteen months). Visiting the sites of the workers' protests in the "small, strike-gripped mining towns — Clifton, Morensi, Ajo, Douglas — strung out across southern Arizona,"[10] Kingsolver became a friend to the group: they trusted her to represent them and their conflict with the mine owners fairly. Kingsolver recalled that she learned by listening: she accumulated shoe boxes of tapes of the conversations, not exactly interviews so much as a "community journal spoken aloud."[11] Knowing these women, seeing their strength amid injustice, and listening to their unique voices, Kingsolver knew she wanted to tell their stories. As she recalled, "I learned the language of Arizona" in these "hundreds and hundreds of hours" of listening to these voices, speaking in their practical and effective mixture of Spanish and English.[12]

Holding the Line: Women in the Great Arizona Mine Strike of 1983 was eventually published in 1989 (and recently brought out again in 1996), but the process of trying to find a publisher for the non-fiction narrative brought Kingsolver to her agent, Frances Goldin, the woman who has advised the writer about all the in's and out's of marketing her work. It also, I think, made Kingsolver realize that she was a very political writer. She found that she wrote best about people with causes, with reasons to take the actions they did, people who acknowledged their own "affect."

After years during her twenties when she had read everything Doris Lessing had written, especially the "Children of Violence" series, Kingsolver began to see the valid connection between hopefulness and politics. Lessing was very influential: "I read everything of Lessing's," she recalls. "I loved the way she evoked Africa. But more than that, maybe on a less conscious level, I loved the fact that she was writing about something real and important — the frustration of women who had absolutely no choices in their lives. . . ."[13] In contrast, as she says on camera, Kingsolver wanted to create fictions where people were enabled to find, and make, choices: "I want people to be hopeful, to think they can change the world."[14] To that end, she repeats,

"I'm a political writer. Why are people terrified about that in the United States?"[15] Dovetailing into her experience covering the Phelps Dodge Corporation Copper strike was the fallout from the Central American and Chilean revolutionary periods, with refugees from political oppression finding safety in the Southwest through the Sanctuary movement. Kingsolver knew some of the refugees; she saw how even shattered lives entertwined, and grew from the support of others better positioned. It exemplified community to her.

Pregnant with her first child, ill, sleeping badly, Kingsolver — typing in a closet so as not to waken her spouse during her insomniac nights — wrote the novel that became *The Bean Trees*. When she sent it to her agent, she had no idea whether the story of Taylor Greer, Kentucky girl headed west, was anything her agent would take on. Goldin quickly saw its value and auctioned the manuscript among the several interested publishing houses. By the time Camille was born, Kingsolver had received a substantial advance check, and in 1988 the novel was on its way to selling over a million copies.

In *The Bean Trees* (a child's description of the pods of wisteria, a plant much more Southern than Southwestern), Kingsolver not only crafts the story of a young, rebellious woman forced into motherhood when a stranger literally gives her a young child in order to save it from horrific abuse. She also extends what is becoming one of her pervasive themes, "How can you be yourself and still be responsible to your community?"[16] In this first novel, Kingsolver's community is mutable, not stable. Taylor has no place to belong. With the child, whom she names Turtle, she creates a home, for herself as well as the child, and she also relies on her friendship with another single parent and her child to form a family. Refugees from Central America (Guatemala) also play a role in the novel. While there is no copper mine strike, Kingsolver is learning to use what surrounds her to build narrative.

To continue to hold reader interest after the surprising success of *The Bean Trees*, Goldin suggested that Kingsolver quickly publish a collection of short stories. *Homeland and Other Stories* appeared in 1989, once again to excellent reviews. The title story was something of a mandala for Kingsolver; she said that she had been conceptualizing—and writing—the story of her Cherokee great-grandmother for fifteen years. The evocative power of the story, for its author, continues. Kingsolver said of it, " 'Homeland' expresses my reason for being as a writer. I hope that story tells about the burden and the joy and the responsibility of holding on to the voices that are getting lost. That's what I want to do as a writer. . . . that's the reason I live."[17]

Like the single story, the collection as a whole gave Kingsolver the chance to perfect her skill using many different voices to create fiction. She did not want everything she wrote after *The Bean Trees* to sound like Taylor Greer; she needed practice in hearing—and then re-creating—other idioms. In the story "Quality Time," for instance, the modern-day mother admits to the strictures of her complicated day; her voice is direct, funny, poignant. In the often-reprinted "Rose-Johnny," Kingsolver uses a more somber style, focusing the reader's attention on the title character's dilemma, as she tries to lead her life of difference in the tiny village of her birth. (First published in *The Virginia Quarterly Review*, this story was produced on stage by Word for Word Theatre Productions, as well as included in *New Stories from the South: The Year's Best*, 1988.) Both contrast with "Homeland," the story which Kingsolver finally had to cut away from its autobiographical root. "The hardest thing to do is write your own history because you're inclined to include all this stuff just because it really happened, not because it adds anything to the story."[18] So she read Cherokee legends for days, "from morning till night, and got a rhythm and a tone of voice in my mind. Then I went back and wrote the sentence, 'My great-grandmother belonged to the Bird Clan.' And I kept that high note all through the story, as far as I could."[19]

In *Animal Dreams*, her second novel, published in 1990, Kingsolver came close to including all the elements she thought made good fiction: interesting characters who were representative of several racial groups; the fusion of plot with theme so that the purpose of the novel seemed realistic, never preachy; a multi-strand narrative (told, in fact, by different speakers, one male, one female); and a wide-scale narrative, which made the novel long, and sometimes difficult to follow. The central characters are sisters, reared by an unsuitably distant doctor-father; the story is told by that male figure and by Codi, the failed medical student, but its heart follows Hallie, the sister who works for peace in Nicaragua. Kingsolver knew she had attempted a great deal. As she explained, the theme of the novel is her recurring one of "seeing ourselves as part of something larger. The individual issues are all aberrations that stem from a central disease of failing to respect the world and our place in it."[20] As it draws a tapestry of strong women (including some who were political activists, despite their usual roles as homemakers), the novel drew heavily on parts of Kingsolver's *Holding the Line*.

A several year grant from the Lila Wallace Foundation enabled Kingsolver and her family to live for a time in Barcelona, as well as in the Canary Islands. Insistent that her young daughter learn to speak another language, Kingsolver was also piqued at the United States involvement in the Gulf War, and considered what she saw as burgeoning imperialism a threat to her life in Arizona. During these years, she wrote and published two books: in 1992, her poem collection, *Another America/Otra America* appeared; the following year, *Pigs in Heaven*, a kind of sequel to *The Bean Trees*. In the case of her poetry, Kingsolver asked her publisher to take a bilingual book. She felt strongly that no single language could express life in a region so mixed linguistically as Arizona is so she designed the book to show each poem, first in English and then, often across the page, that poem translated into Spanish by the Chilean writer Rebeca Cartes. It was a two-language book: it was intended for the bilingual reader as well as the general reader. And it was angry. Kingsolver calls her poems "little steam vents on the pressure cooker," and notes that while there are strong emotions evident in her fiction, in the poems—which have emotional response as a base—the emotions take precedence over the art form.[21]

With *Pigs in Heaven*, she felt that she had the opportunity to return to the Native American culture she had looked at in both her first novels (sometimes being criticized for her use of a culture she didn't understand as thoroughly as she might), and give it fuller depiction and dynamic. Exploring native cultures this time from the inside out, after much more study and investigation, Kingsolver felt that her "anthropologist's heart" had helped her write a novel that was more true to the culture and the people she dealt with in the on-going struggle for Turtle's creation of a home. Like Kingsolver, Taylor Greer was learning quickly.

In 1995, Kingsolver published a collection of her essays and occasional pieces. Most publishers avoid bringing out such books because essays sell poorly; but *High Tide in Tucson* sold very well, even in hard cover. The phenomenon of a Kingsolver book being a best-seller continued. That same year she was awarded an Honorary Doctorate of Letters by her undergraduate school, De Pauw University.

Divorced for several years, able to support her family well from her writing, and back in the United States, Barbara Kingsolver continued doing the kinds of tasks highly successful writers are obligated to do. She went on book tours; she gave interviews; she read on campuses, and spent days in residence meeting with students and faculty. One of the people she met during this period of her life was Steven Hopp, a teacher and a guitarist. They married and created a compatible life in Arizona, and in 1996 she had a second daughter, Lily. Perhaps complete with the existence of a loving and secure family, Kingsolver continued to work toward the novel that she had spent part of the past three years conceiving and preparing for. *The Poisonwood Bible* would be the novel that brought Kingsolver into the purview of a wider literary establishment; in the words of a *New York Times* critic, Sarah Kerr, it would be her "quantum-leap breakthrough."[22]

As Kingsolver described the process, it was necessarily lengthy. Aside from her family's visit during 1963 and the photographs and memories of her parents during that time, she had no experience at all with African culture. Several trips into Western and Central Africa (which was as near as she could get to Mobutu's Zaire) gave her the rich detail about country, vegetation, and life; living with families in those areas (and doing the marketing, cooking, and tending children) gave her account realism. While she had read and studied in libraries and museums in the States (and the novel includes a bibliography of particularly helpful sources), the authenticity Kingsolver achieved came from her personal immersion in the country and its culture.

She didn't simplify the difficulties of preparing to write. As she wrote once the book had appeared, "Historical fiction is a frightening labor-intensive proposition. . . . I read a lot of books about the political, social, and natural history of Africa and the Congo. . . . Sometimes, reading a whole, densely-written book on, say, the formation and dissolution of indigenous political parties during the Congolese independence, or an account of the life histories of Central African venomous snakes, would move me only a sentence or two forward in my understanding of my subject. But every sentence mattered."[23]

Kingsolver also read widely in the King James Bible, so as to understand "the rhythm of the Price family's speech, the frame of reference for their beliefs, and countless plot ideas." But most important to her understanding of the Congolese languages, she read "a huge old two-volume Kikongo-French dictionary, compiled early in the century (by a missionary, of course). Slowly I began to grasp the music and subtlety of this amazing African language, with its infinite capacity for being misunderstood and mistranslated."[24]

There is a great deal to say about this long account of a comparatively innocent family from the United States who followed their father's messianic zeal to go to the Belgian Congo and Christianize the heathen natives. It is a story as old as time: the possession of the untaught and unlettered (and something other than Christian) by the righteous preacher, who is educated, saved, and white. In King-solver's words, it is a story about people, cultures, conflict and, particularly, about "cultural imperialism and post-colonial history."[25]

2

The Novel

Barbara Kingsolver's 1998 novel may well prove to be one of the most important books of the 1990s. The work can easily be classified as postcolonial: it shows the erroneously proprietary assumptions of the white missionary family, particularly the minister Nathan Price, as he forces his way into the small Congo village which his own ministry warns him away from. The year is 1959, and the threat of Congolese independence has already sent most Europeans and Americans back to their home countries. Belgium is ready to relinquish control of its territory. Yet Nathan, a poorly educated Georgia Baptist with no training for assuming leadership within the African culture, declares himself the chosen one and takes his wife, Orleanna, and four young daughters into the dangerous land.

Kingsolver's subtle handling of the actual historical events of the first five years of Congolese struggle — complete with the narratives of Patrice Lumumba, Joseph Mobutu, Moise Tshombe, and their partisans — never undercuts her emphasis on the Price family and their struggle against the unfamiliar in the African wild. In many works characterized as postcolonial, the national narrative takes precedence over the personal.

The Poisonwood Bible is also a feminist novel. Kingsolver's defi-
nition of patriarchy, though seemingly institutional and embedded
in and reinforced through religion, is essentially based on the family. By combining Nathan's patriarchal authority as husband and
father with his less questionable role as religious leader, Kingsolver
sets for her readers the same dilemma his wife and daughters face:
how to separate Nathan Price, the abusive spouse and parent, from
Nathan Price, chosen minister of God's word. Using the narrative
sections of Leah, the most generous of the four daughters, Kingsolver shows the gradual change in the family's perception of their
father: Nathan changes from being a modest World War II hero
(bothered by his unknown "war injury") to "a small befuddled
stranger,"[1] defeated by his failure to harvest—either food or souls—
in the Congolese climate. As his sometimes hidden anger builds to
mind-destroying fury, Nathan unleashes the self-hatred of his irrep-
arable war wound—his guilt at being the one man to live through
the brutal devastation of World War II. Using Nathan to show the
theme of war as wound, and wounding, strengthens Kingsolver's
narrative of the Congo's fight for national independence, a fight
that will inevitably foment destruction. Again, the impersonality of
war is translated—vividly—through the story of the human waste it
inevitably creates.

The way in which Kingsolver chooses to tell the Price family's
story gives her options that keep readers sheltered for a while from
the enormity of the truth about Nathan's unfortunate mania. The
novel is both metaphoric and structurally difficult. The metaphor
occurs in that she tells the story through its religiosity, a strategy that
compels the reader to ask questions that themselves undermine
patriarchal authority—for instance, reflective of the novel's tena-
cious Biblical overtones, what is "the pearl of great price" that
Nathan Price is willing to trade the well-being of his family to
obtain? (The repetition of the family name drills this Biblical phrase

into the reader's consciousness.) More obviously, what is the title riddle, this "poisonwood Bible"? How does the Bible, sacrosanct in its authoritative power as Bible, become *bangala*, dangerous, powerful enough to annihilate, (i.e., poisonwood)?

To reinforce the reader's attention on the Biblical emphasis, Kingsolver opens each of the novel's seven books with a quotation from either the King James Bible or the Apocrypha, allowing the reader to build a subjective understanding of what the often elliptical verses "mean." The first epigraph, for instance, is Genesis 1:28: "And God said unto them,/ Be fruitful, and multiply, and replenish the earth,/ and subdue it: and have dominion/ over the fish of the sea, and over the fowl of the air,/ and over every living thing that moveth upon the earth" both justifies a father's use of his progeny and challenges his power to control "every living thing" (p. 1). Taken ironically, the verse is transformed from the pacific reasonableness the world expects to become a paean to the usurpation of everything alive: the real text of Genesis 1:28 is power. The reader soon discovers that Nathan Price does not ever intend to share what power he has.

To open the second book of the novel, Kingsolver chooses Revelation 13: 1, 9: "And I stood upon the sand of the sea,/ and saw a beast rise up. . . . / If any man have an ear, let him hear" (p. 83). As Orleanna's meditation that follows the passage makes clear, she has just begun to see her spouse's depravity. Nathan is the "beast" that the speaker sees "rise up." What consequences her new sight will have, in this rigidly patriarchal marriage, will be brutal.

For Book Three, Kingsolver chooses as epigraph Judges 2:2–3, a passage that speaks more directly to the Congolese plight. "And ye shall make no league with the/ inhabitants of this land;/ ye shall throw down their altars . . . / They shall be as thorns in your sides,/ and their gods shall be a snare unto you" (p. 187). In trampling the Congolese beliefs underfoot, rather than trying to incorporate them into Christianity, Nathan Price has literally followed this precept, but he has not considered whose words he is heeding. Unfortunately, he has self-righteously thrown down their altars; he does duel with their gods. Taking the Bible and the situation as ironic brings the reader more fully into Orleanna's own questioning of Nathan's decisions. It is Orleanna's heart of darkness the reader uncovers. She finally has no choice but to leave her husband, to recognize his madness.

This narrative technique of centering the various books of the novel, some of them nearly one hundred pages long, on a single opening verse is more than a narrative tour de force, however, because the strategy is rooted in Nathan Price's psychosis: his consistent punishment for his four daughters, chosen with specific meanness, is to assign each of them "the verse." Whenever any of the four displeases him, he chooses a verse to which she must copy out the one hundred verses that precede it: a prolegomenon of guilt that finally brings the daughter to the single verse, her father's "word." The words may literally be those from the Bible, but the choice, and the emphatic "last word," is that of Nathan Price. The punishment is his, not God's. Such a travesty of education — children, particularly young children, should learn to find comfort in Bible stories — shows Nathan's need to usurp power from all sources; Nathan is a spoiler, not a cherisher.

In a dramatic style reminiscent of the method William Faulkner used in his novel *As I Lay Dying*, Kingsolver sets up an intricate seven-book structure composed of more than a hundred narrative segments spoken in turn by each of the four daughters — Rachel, the oldest, is a flighty teenager; Adah and Leah are incompatible twins; Ruth May is a pre-schooler. Each child's name appears at the head of her section. This named narrator convention is the primary vehicle of the story.

Each of the seven books of the novel follows the same structural pattern. First comes the bible verse. After each opening epigraph

comes the mother's—Orleanna Price's—opening meditation, a segment that does not become a part of the narration proper but rather
creates a poetic tone and in some cases an image for the segmented
narratives of the four daughters to come. While Orleanna's meditation does combine a sense of the wife and mother's guilt and
responsibility for their being in Africa at all, with the characterization of the young Georgia woman who has married Nathan Price,
with little recognition of either his limits or those of the church, it
also serves as a kind of tonal organ base for the book. What Kingsolver presents to the reader, then, is a narrative of four separate
speaker-observers—all of them Nathan's and Orleanna's daughters—
hinged to, and painfully wrung from, the monologue of their
mother. The father has no voiced sections of his own: he appears
only as a character within his wife's and his children's stories.

The structure of the novel, then, creates a story that is much
more gendered than it might at first appear. Yes, the entire family
is ignorant of the Congolese culture into which it goes; the women
make as many obtuse mistakes as their father, and many of the same
kind of mistakes. But implicit in each daughter's account is the
unquestioned power of the father (the cynical Adah refers to Nathan
as "Our Father"), and the resultingly inconsequential lives his wife
and children are forced to lead. The Price women are literally
without price because, in Nathan's eyes, they are worthless. The
indeterminacy within *The Poisonwood Bible*, the ambivalence that
gives the events of the book more than their obvious effect, stems
from Kingsolver's striking convention of choosing as narrators of the
story characters who are shown to be, initially, powerless. Never
didactic, the novel marches ahead much less often than it strolls in
a circular path. With each curve, the reader becomes more and
more engrossed in not only the happenings of the work, but the
way each narrator manages to meet, withstand, and perhaps grow
from those events.

One of Kingsolver's skills as novelist lies in her magical differentiation of the narrating characters. There is the pathetic Orleanna, the thoroughly discouraged mother whose guilt for loving her husband has eaten her almost into death. There is the oldest daughter Rachel, beloved for her impatience, her vanity, and her malapropisms. There are the gifted twins Leah and Adah, each trapped by the accident of birth in an adversarial role to the other. And there is Ruth May, the youngest and sweetest of the daughters. Leah becomes the voice of faith: she wants to be a man like her father Nathan, she has a confidence about his decisions that is difficult to shake, she tries to become learned, open-minded, kind. Ruth May is the essential of hope. It is she who breaks through the tough language barrier and teaches the young Congolese to play "Mother, May I?" with her and her sisters. Curious, impetuous, and consistently loving, Ruth May is understandably the best beloved of the four girls.

Neither Adah nor Rachel, despite their names, is marked by charity. Adah, embittered about her congenital illness, sees her misshapen body — in tandem with her brilliant yet cynical mind — as the work of Ham. She is the child who will never fit, the daughter who will never be beautiful. Accordingly, she turns away from Nathan, just as he turns away from her and sees her as a physical manifestation of a devilish counterpart. For Nathan to be inordinately close to Leah, her twin, and never concerned about Adah is the most cruel of Nathan's choices. In punishment of his choice, and in punishment of her family's failure to compensate for Nathan's cruelty, Adah does not speak: her silent interior monologue in its schizoid brilliance has a great many elements of humor, made even more precious because only Adah and the reader are privy to them.

In the character of Rachel, Kingsolver creates a product that is purely American female, a 1950s adolescent on the make for a proper husband. Nothing more taxing than her clothes and hairstyle holds Rachel's attention. Oblivious to the social and political conditions of the Congolese, Rachel does become the one thing of value in the Price family. In her pristine blonde beauty, her color-free ambience, Rachel becomes the pearl of the family: her only ambition, to marry well, nearly saves the Prices from the devastation that they finally experience. But there is no charity within Rachel, nor is there any self-knowledge, even as the reader sees her later in the novel after her fiftieth birthday, still a predator on the African economic culture. Her name is but a travesty of the Biblical Rachel, long beloved by Jacob, who was tricked by Rachel's father to marry her sister Leah instead. Kingsolver gives the reader the alliance between Leah and Nathan (whose name echoes that of Laban, Rachel's father), but decimates Rachel's character as loving partner and eventual mother. Rachel Price bears no children.

Most of Kingsolver's efforts to have her four protagonists grow and change, hopefully becoming responsive to the struggles of the Congo as their larger model, achieve little visible drama. As if continually reminding the reader that little freedom is possible, whether these women live in the States or in the Congo, Kingsolver works within the conventions of women's lives — what are the roles of obedient daughters? What are the roles of obedient wives? One of the reasons the history of the Congo struggle for independence is so muted, almost hidden, in *The Poisonwood Bible* is that any attempt to gain freedom — from any dictator or any patriarch — jars against the submission expected from the family of Nathan and his five women. To keep the novel in the hands of its human subjects must be to keep its emotional tone static.

There is a reason Jo March, from Louisa May Alcott's 1868 novel *Little Women*, is mentioned here: in a hundred years, the lives of good women in the United States had changed very little. In Alcott's fiction, the March daughters, all four of them, remain submissive to their father—a minister who serves humankind during the Civil War—but their loving Marmee seems more capable than does Orleanna, when we first meet her through her meditations from Sanderling Island. The March sisters also are not faced with cultural otherness, deprivation of any real magnitude, or a need to break with the social mandates under which they have matured. Comparison between Alcott's *Little Women*, whose title at least names the daughters' life experiences, and Kingsolver's *The Poisonwood Bible*, with its ostensible focus on the Price family's earnest mission to Africa, shows in part how small the world has become, and, perhaps accordingly, how complex the nature of changing roles for women has become.

BOOK ONE:

"The Things We Carried"

Like all good novels, *The Poisonwood Bible* has a starting point. As the Price family gets ready for its journey from Georgia to Africa, the family focus is on what objects of their daily life they can take with them to the Congo. With Kingsolver's emphasis on Orleanna's bringing cake mixes, one for each person's birthday, she disarms the political reader: the "things" of her story are intimate parts of this six-person family's existence. The anger in Rachel's narrative, the pretension in Leah's—with her aim to conquer not only the various African languages but as many of their cultures, the wistfulness in Ruth May's childish sense of change, and the bitterness in Adah's having to face her physical disabilities in a less convenient place keeps the reader off guard. The foreboding of living in the Congo becomes the pique of individual girls; again, Kingsolver's emphasis on each daughter's packing makes the narrative into four personal sagas. But the real sense of foreboding occurs in Orleanna's meditation, which opens with the imperative sentence: "Imagine a ruin so strange it must never have happened."

Inexplicable to the reader here at the start of the book proper. What ruin? The first sentence after this is the opening of a standard paragraph, yet it too — again an imperative — is elliptical: "First, picture the forest. I want you to be its conscience, the eyes in the trees." Once the lush equatorial jungle is imprinted in the reader's mind, Orleanna presents the tonal key to the entire novel. This is the opening of the second paragraph:

Away down below now, single file on the path, comes a woman with four girls in tow, all of them in shirtwaist dresses. Seen from above this way they are pale, doomed blossoms, bound to appeal to your sympathies. Be careful. Later on you'll have to decide what sympathy they deserve.... (p. 5)

No *Little Women* here, but rather the clear knell of impending tragedy. Yet, in the postmodern style so appropriate to the genre of postcolonial narrative, Orleanna makes her characterization mutable: young and, we suppose, blighted women deserve reader sympathy — except that as soon as Orleanna's voice suggests that plot line, she qualifies our extending sympathy. She does the same thing with her own persona: "The mother especially — watch how she leads them on, pale-eyed, deliberate." A hesitant kind of guilt, an amorphous sense of self: in this her first meditation, her introduction of her character and her narrative to its reader, Orleanna redeems only the natural world. The mother, distraught to the point of despair, witnesses the rare appearance of a male okapi, the unicorn supposedly to be tamed only by a virgin, the mythic one-horned figure of legend. Orleanna's okapi becomes her totem, what remains of her years in Africa, what remains of her self.

As she had in her second novel, *Animal Dreams*, Kingsolver makes Orleanna's meditation — as she does much of the novel proper — a study of motherhood and the sacrifices, and the strange prides, it entails. Within Orleanna's first section are such key statements as "One has *only* a life of one's own" (to contrast with the stereotypical notion that mothers give all of themselves to mothering and consequently have "no life" for themselves) and "I married a man who could never love me, probably." (p. 8) She also admits that none of her family needed her, not even the younger children, though the narrative contradicts this assessment. The contrived but effective absence of love (i.e., charity) in the novel makes it the antithesis of the Bible, at least of the New Testament, where all Christ's teachings return to the concept of loving another as oneself.

Orleanna's brutal monologue does more than characterize the wife and mother of the American family, however. It draws that family into the postcolonial context, seemingly without self-consciousness. Africa is the theater for the Price family drama, an Africa to which the family brings only ignorance and arrogance. In the opening of Orleanna's section, she uses the image of the mother and children forcing a path through the jungle for an unsatisfying picnic beside the river. The journey is hard; the mother "leads the way, parting curtain after curtain of spiders' webs. She appears to be conducting a symphony. Behind them the curtain closes. The spiders return to their killing ways." (p. 6) Like Orleanna's effect on her family, her impact on Africa is fleeting, inconsequential.

Orleanna's being in Africa is not entirely her husband's fault; she acknowledges her own guilt, "I walked across Africa with my wrists unshackled. . . . I trod on Africa without a thought, straight from our family's divinely inspired beginning to our terrible end." (p.9) Beyond her statements of fact, however metaphoric, the reader hears her pained concept of fortune, value, price: "Some of us know how we came by our fortune, and some of us don't, but we wear it all the same. There's only one question worth asking now: How do we aim to live with it?. . . . I know people. Most have no earthly notion of the price of a snow-white conscience." (p. 9)

From her retirement space on Sanderling Island off the coast of Georgia, Orleanna has come to recognize the fallacy of self-righteous belief, especially that which privileges her husband's kind of Christianity. She has touched the depths of despair: "She is inhumanly alone," she says of the Orleanna Price on the riverbank. But at that moment of reckoning, the vision that appears to her is not a burning bush or an angel; it is rather the lone okapi, the elusive African beast. *Her* unicorn. *Her* blessing, *her* miracle.

The eleven sections of the various daughters' monologues present the Price family's first months in Kilanga. Book I, despite its four narrators and disparate events, works as a unit to show Nathan Price's utter ignorance of his Congolese parishioners: at their impressive arrival feast for the Prices, he censures the people for their nakedness, refusing to see that in their poverty and their lifestyle, Western clothing is the rarest of luxuries — and unnecessary as well. His contriving to celebrate Easter in early July — denying the validity of the Congolese calendar as well as the Christian one — is another mark of his disdain, and the triumph he visualizes of his baptizing the village's children on that festival day (along with his own youngest daughter) turns to defeat. No one will enter the river, the planned site of his ceremony. Only at the end of the book does Nathan (and the reader) learn that one of the village children was recently eaten by crocodiles in that river: his frustration when he discovers this leads to his anger, that no one has told him. Impaired by his own lack of language, unable to listen to anyone who tries to communicate with him (including his own wife and children), and — worse — unwilling to try to listen to anyone, Nathan has by the end of Book I fired the one Congolese household helper, Mama Bekwa Tataha, and set free the parrot (a house pet who is killed quickly), who was their link with the former minister. He has also, by disregarding Mama Tataha's advice, been ill because of his encounter with the poisonwood plant.

The narrative sections open with Leah's first segment. The clearest, and firmest, of the daughers' voices, Leah's is fired with her admiration for her father. She is his chosen child, the sidekick who will inherit whatever his power grows to be: she basks in her privileged position. Her surety lets her speak humorously: "We came from Bethlehem, Georgia, bearing Betty Crocker cake mixes into the jungle." (p. 13) Yet the substance of her section shows the relative power of her parents, and the position of the other daughters: she leaves no question about the absence of equality. She introduces Reverend and Mrs. Underdown, the Baptists who had recently left the post they were to have, there at the Leopoldville airport to help the Prices through customs and to send them to Kilanga by small plane. And she describes their arrival after landing: "We stood blinking for a moment, staring out through the dust at a hundred dark villagers, slender and silent, swaying faintly like trees. We'd left Georgia at the height of a peach-blossom summer and now stood in a bewildering dry, red fog that seemed like no particular season you could put your finger on." (p. 18)

Kingsolver contrasts Leah's informed voice with the second section, Ruth May's trying to figure out why Africans are dark-skinned. In her connection with the tribes of Ham, and her confusion with Donald Duck, Lone Ranger, and Cinderella, she is touchingly bewildered by the strangeness of the composition of the village. One of her paragraphs begins, "Here are the other white people we had in Africa so far." (p. 21) Coming from segregated Georgia, dominated by what Ruth May calls "Jimmy Crow," her responses to "the colored children" are as logical as Leah's tendency to assimilate to Kilanga culture.

Ready for the comedy of Rachel's confused language (she begins by describing the feast as a "pandemony," and notes that she is "in the sloop of despond"), the reader is again faced with the task of interpreting what language means. It is Rachel's account of her father's terrible insults to the Congolese (about their nakedness, their heathen ways) that lets the reader see she is not exaggerating when she closes her segment with the hyperbolic, "I wept for the sins of all who had brought my family to this dread dark shore." (p. 29)

Adah Price is the genius narrator, fond of puns, language games, and distilled commentary. She also quickly becomes the reader's mind. She says directly what the reader intuits; she provides objective information but her punning takes some of the sting from it. "Sunrise tantalize, evil eyes hypnotize: that is the morning, Congo pink. . . . A wide red plank of dirt—the so-called road—flat-out in front of us, continuous in theory from here to somewhere distant. But the way I see it through my Adah eyes it is a flat plank clipped into pieces, rectangles and trapezoids, by the skinny black-line shadows of tall palm trunks." (p. 30) Protected by her own silence, Adah is free to observe the dynamics of both the family and the people of the Congo. Most of the time, she is able to stay away from her father; but in her chosen loneliness, she comes to mirror her physically misshapen young body. There is no joy in Adah's life, but there is the ability to scrutinize.

Even in this first book, Kingsolver makes clear that the most honest assessments of the family life will come from anyone but Leah. Blinded by her admiration for Nathan, Leah recounts her father's acts positively. It is from Adah's acerbic narratives, Rachel's confrontational ones, and Ruth May's innocent stories that the more complete picture grows: only Orleanna's gift to the Congolese of fried chicken at the "Easter" celebration has kept the congregation placid; only her desire to have her daughters learn the language and customs keeps them intent on making a life in the Congo. It is difficult to imagine any survival without Orleanna, yet when Mama Tataha leaves, Orleanna becomes little but the family servant. The sheer work of finding and preparing food, chopping wood, bringing water, building fires, doing laundry, bathing—the primitive life without help threatens to kill not only her spirit but her body. The several instances of Orleanna "talking back" to Nathan in Book I show the fear the family feels in relation to their father; in every case, Orleanna is trying to explain the Congolese to her spouse. But whatever she says is at her own bodily peril.

BOOK II:

"The Things We Learned"

The hopeful reader expects that it will be Nathan Price who has some kind of revelation, being guided by the opening epigraph; but instead the verse bears only an ironic relationship to the tone of Orleanna's second meditation. In it she describes her hatred for the sense of Africa's lushness, its dark mystery, but more importantly, her hatred of her own vacillation about her role in the Congo: "I'd thought I could have it both ways: to be one of them, and also my husband's wife. What conceit! I was his instrument, his animal. Nothing more." (p. 89) The bitterness of her revelation—crystallized with Nathan's diabolical destruction of the only beautiful thing in their house, the delicate white serving platter—leads her to condemn her condition, that of wife: "I was just one more of those women who clamp their mouths shut and wave the flag as their nation rolls off to conquer another in war. . . . They *are* what there is to lose. A wife is the earth itself, changing hands, bearing scars." (p. 89)

Slowly, Kingsolver brings the politics of Congolese independence into the narrative; in Orleanna's lament above, she becomes a colonized object—metaphorically, the reader has been introduced to national/masculine possession. Generally, however, Kingsolver keeps the reader's attention on the Price family story, although she begins to introduce Congolese politics through the character of Anatole, the young African school teacher who also is supposed to translate Nathan's sermons.

What the author does not do is provide a chronology of political events for the reader. Instead, she builds *The Poisonwood Bible* on the human ramifications of the country's internal conflicts. For Anatole and the men of his generation, their lives become double. Conspirators at night, they have to maintain their normal lives; they cover each other's absences. To help the Price family, Anatole provides them with young boys, those too young to be involved in the fighting.

The irony of the congruence of Congolese independence and Nathan Price's usurpation of power occurs in the novel largely through innuendo. While the Prices were stunned by what surrounded them in Kilanga, the Congo was struggling to become independent. In May of 1960, Patrice Lumumba and Joseph Kasavubu shared power—for a week. Army units mutinied, nearly all Europeans left. While Nathan Price was working to prepare the "Easter" service (on July 4, 1960), the Congo had declared its independence on June 30. When government quickly broke down, it asked the United Nations for help. In July, 1960, the rich diamond area, Katanga province, under Moise Tshombe, declared itself an independent country. United Nations troops started arriving July 15, 1960, and remined until June 30, 1964.

September 5, 1960, President Kasavubu dismissed Lumumba. Joseph Mobutu, army colonel, set up a provisional government made up of university students at Leopoldville, now named Kinshasa. Lumumba was imprisoned but his followers set up a rival government at Stanleyville, now named Kisangani; their leader was Antoine Gizenga. Other provinces declared independence; by November, 1960, there were four rival governments in the Congo. In January of 1961, the popular Lumumba—who would have probably been able to unify the country—was assassinated in Katanga.

Just as life in Kilanga went on with apparently little notice of the political (and life-threatening) conflict, Kingsolver's novel continues on its way to provide the intricate dimensions of the Price family story. The daughters' sections in Book II state and then embroider the theme of the inability of one culture to understand the language of another. Book II is a group of sections rich in illustrations of the way language can open discourse, or close it tightly. Here, Adah's seemingly idiosyncratic musings on her hemiplegia (asymmetrical brain, as in Wernicke's and Broca's aphasia) move into a central position in the narrative. That Adah sees language differently, that she sees words as a means to play, becomes one way into the strangely incomprehensible Congolese dialects. Her sentences of words linked through sound patterns and rhyme ("the drear monosyllabic Ade, lemonade, Band-Aid, frayed blockade, switchblade renegade, call a spade a spade") convey a logic of their own: "I prefer *Ada* as it goes either way, like me. I am a perfect Palindrome. *Damn mad!* Across the cover of my notebook I have written as a warning to others:

ELAPSED OR ESTEEMED, ALL ADE MEETS ERODES PALE!"

As she concludes, "The Congo is a fine place to learn how to read the same book many times." (pp. 57–58)

Leah's approach is more literal and more painstaking. With Anatole and her younger friend Pascal's help, she will conquer the language Kikongo, even though a single word may have dissimilar meanings. *Nzolo*, for example, depending on its inflection, can mean "most dearly beloved"—or a thick yellow grub, or a tiny potato. *Dundu*, a word for price, also is an antelope, a small plant, or a hill. But despite the complications of misheard language, Book

II through the interaction between Leah and Anatole begins to convey the sense of the Congo as battleground — the young Congolese, being trained by Anatole and others, set against the European/ Belgian and mercenary forces. When Ruth May breaks her arm and is taken by plane to Stanleyville, the doctor's conversation about Patrice Lumumba is the first open discussion Nathan Price hears. When the Underdowns come to urge the Price family to leave — to insist that they must leave, the political situation is clarified further, as is some history of the Congo under brutal Belgium rule. As the country grows more militant, more conscious of its degrading poverty under white rule, the villagers grow more aggressive toward the Prices. There are gifts of food, but there are also dangerous acts: a poisonous snake planted in a bedroom, congregation members warned away from church. Nelson, the young househelper Anatole has sent them, provides both history and alternative beliefs, urging Ruth May in the early stages of the illness that becomes malaria, to adopt her own *gree-gree*, the totem of her personal African god. The reader, like the Price family, has begun to lose patience with the steadfastness of Nathan Price. In his brutality to Orleanna, his striking Leah, his stubborn refusal to leave the Congo, he has proven Rachel's somewhat flip assessment to be accurate:

Father stared at the trees, giving no indication he'd heard his poor frightened wife, or any of this news. Father would sooner watch us all perish one by one than listen to anybody but himself. (p. 169)

When the rescue plane arrives, however, the family does not leave. Only Nathan Price and Leah get aboard. He and his favorite daughter will travel to hear the speeches at the June 30, 1960, Congolese independence ceremony. They will observe Patrice Lumumba, and draw their own conclusions. But they will return to the Price ministry.

In despair and fear, Orleanna Price and Ruth May take to bed. They do not get up for many weeks. Sick as they are with malaria, Nathan considers their illness to be betrayal and does not care for them. As Kingsolver presents the long, wearying illness, the physical state of the family members becomes a metaphor for the dysfunction of the unit; the responsibility for curing the sick rests with Nathan, who does nothing. His ministry is shown to be as ineffectual within the family as it is outside it.

BOOK III:

"The Things We Didn't Know"

Even as the frame of successful self-government crumbles, with Lumumba's arrest and imprisonment, so life within the Price household bears little resemblance to what it had been only brief weeks earlier. Distraught with the powerlessness of her role as wife and mother, faced with the blatant cruelty for which there is no excuse, in her third monologue Orleanna speaks directly about Nathan. Regretfully, she calls him a man "who simply can see no way to have a daughter but to own her like a plot of land, to work her, plow her under, rain down a dreadful poison upon her." Once again, the theme of this meditation is her love for her deprived children but here Orleanna emphasizes that she is complicit as his wife, a mother who has no recourse: "It was you who let him plant it [the devil's seed, his seed]." (p. 191)

In her acceptance of her inferiority, her boundedness by sex, her guilt, Orleanna seems to excuse Nathan as she retraces his devastating war experience. Wounded, he is hospitalized and not yet returned to his company in the Pacific. But once he learns of that unit's fate on the Death March from Bataan, she thinks, his soul dies. At home after recovering from his war injuries, Nathan becomes the abusive man she has known since, and she concludes about his drivenness: "He meant personally to save more souls than had perished on the road from Bataan . . . and all other paths ever walked by the blight of mankind." (p. 198) The passion of Nathan's guilty righteousness suggests scholar Carolyn Marvin's belief that "Religion organizes killing energy. More precisely, it organizes men who wish to kill so they will kill the right people."[2]

Orleanna's monologue returns to her own soul, however, and she traces her process of enlightenment to her taking "a long time to understand the awful price I'd paid." Like Africa, her bondage to a white oppressor could be broken only with force. The emotional core is provided early in Book III by Ruth May's quiet comment to her mother, in Nathan's absence: "Mama, I hope he never comes back" (p. 215).

Just as Orleanna was coming to understanding in the sick bed she shared with her youngest daughter, so was the Congo in its throes of struggle. But the Prices, for all intents and purposes, remained blind to the real dangers of those throes: their position as white people could no longer be seen as helpful, or even as neutral. Real information comes to the family through Leah, by way of the dangerously-involved Anatole, whose own wisdom enables him to help the Prices learn enough to stay safe. Nathan Price is as blind as he is deaf, however, and were it not for the kindness of their poor neighbors, the Prices might not survive. (Survival as Kingsolver first describes it is on a subsistence level: with Orleanna bedfast, the daughters try to find, and prepare, food, but it is a losing battle. The discomfort of sheer hunger, always underscored with Nathan's beatings when what food there is is inedible, changes to the discomfort of the reader's realization of emotional abandonment.)

From the spying of Adah and Ruth May and the self-interested observations of Rachel, the reader knows that Eeben Axelroot, the surly reprehensible pilot, is a counter-revolutionary. Smuggling diamonds and other valuables, providing a radio link to the mercenary forces, he has become rich during the brief Congolese conflict. Now, when the Price family is faced with an unbelievable situation — that Rachel is being courted by the village witch doctor (a man who is so wealthy he already has a number of wives), Axelroot offers to take Rachel off their hands. His argument is that if she is engaged to him, she can no longer be courted by Tata Ndu. Here is one turning point for the novel: if Nathan cares so little for his daughter that he lets her become the sexual booty of this criminal, he is lost to the civilized world. He is also lost to Africa. No father would allow this exchange.

Kingsolver writes this series of events with a level of understatement that plays the reader's usual lack of sympathy for Rachel against the horror of the situation. A central book in the novel, this indictment of the father who would pass judgment on everyone and everything, only to do nothing to prevent the destruction of his own child, Book III ("The Judges") shifts the interest in *The Poisonwood Bible* from family history and historical political events to philosophical balance. The twenty-two sections of narrative here are truly incremental. They do much more than move the narrative from point to point; there is much repetition within the segments told by the four daughter narrators. Ruth May, in her delirium, recounts Rachel's being knocked down by Nathan as she tries to run away from the house and forge her own escape. Adah and Leah join together to describe Tata Ndu's courtship. Rachel describes her alienation from her parents.

The focus in Book III is on Rachel and her betrayal by her family, but the details of the courtship and her sense of abandonment are layered throughout several segments. The quiet accumulation of these details gives the reader time to recognize the enormity of what is happening to Rachel. If the promise of the young American woman is to make a successful marriage, as the

Christmas hope chest scenes have suggested, then Rachel has truly been sold out.

The author's unusual choice of humor to portray the Congolese belief in a woman's physical and sexual preparation for marriage — "circus mission," as Ruth May describes vaginal/labial circumcision — underscores the real danger Rachel faces. Ruth May's cryptic monologue lists the various dangers for white women in the Congo: the rapes and murders now occurring in politically divided Stanleyville, with special danger for white women; her understanding of the way Rachel would have to be "cut . . . so she wouldn't want to run around with people's husbands"; and her insightful dream of patriarchal power that "it is Father she's marrying and I get mixed up and sad. Because then: where is Mama?" (p. 271) Ruth May also recounts the severe arguments Nathan and Orleanna have over this bartering for Rachel. According to Ruth May, "she said her first job was to take care of her own and if he was any kind of a father he would do the same." Effective in its indirection, Ruth May's childish monologue clearly points the direction for Nathan to assume responsibility. But he takes no action at all.

Instead, Nathan plays the race card. To argue against Orleanna's insistence that he protect Rachel, still at this point a child of sixteen, he chooses to let her be taken by Axelroot — after all, "white people have to stick together," in Ruth May's paraphrase. (p. 273) For the reader, such an allegiance is only the sign of Nathan's naivete. Kingsolver has already made plain (through Axelroot's bragging to Rachel) that he is a murderer, a hired gun, "a flying fighter. How he has shot very influential men in cold blood and dropped fire bombs from the air that can burn up a whole field of crops in ten seconds flat. He's not just an errand boy flying missionaries around. . . ." (p. 270)

To unify the book, once Rachel's hand has been given to Axelroot, he brags some more, and it is at the ending of Book III that he tells her about the coming assassination of Lumumba, that he is "as good as dead." Speaking of the radio message he had intercepted, and using the code names that peppered his conversation, he told Rachel "Devil One was supposed to get his so-called operatives to convince the army men to go against Lumumba. Supposedly this Devil One person was going to get one million dollars from the United States to pay soldiers to do that, go against the very person they all just elected. A million dollars!" (p. 294)

True to her ability to interweave the separate strands of her narrative, Kingsolver waits until a few sections later to return to the issue of Nathan Price's guilt. In Adah's section, she tries to discuss with her father the Congolese women's feelings for the many children who have died from the summer's illnesses. It is Nathan's conclusion that "the Congolese do not become attached to their children as we Americans do." (p. 297) His research has been based on his conversations with the bereaved women (although he knows none of their dialects), and Adah, who has herself observed a number of the African children's funerals, mocks his scientific work with these sentences: "Oh, a man of the world is Our Father. He is writing a learned article on this subject for the Baptist scholars back home." (p. 297) Seemingly separate from what has happened to Rachel, this segment of plot strikes home with a bitter irony.

Adah is also the purveyor of pieces of political information. Leah knows what Anatole tells her, but Adah moves about the jungle at night, her most frequent site Axelroot's cabin and its radio transmissions. The cabin is also visited by other men as the political activity increases. Through Adah's observations, and through Axelroot's bragging to Rachel, the reader learns how complicit the United States is in the plan to overthrow Lumumba. But just as it seems that *The Poisonwood Bible* is about to become a full-blown historical account of Congolese struggle, a plague of ants attacks. Biblical in its horror, this unexpected plague makes the narrative move quickly again, but it also makes Orleanna determine ways to save her children. Kingsolver casts the reader back into the dilemma of the mother's responsibility creating a conundrum: which child can she carry? Neither Ruth May nor Adah can walk fast enough to make it to the Kwilu River; Orleanna cannot carry both.

African friends rescue them. When Leah is being cared for by Anatole, she recognizes that the Prices are so out of place, so much trouble, that they should never have come to Africa. "We're just fools that have gotten by so far on dumb luck. . . . We shouldn't have come."

"No, you shouldn't. But you are here, so yes, you should be here. There are more words in the world than no and yes," Anatole replies.

"You're the only one here who'll even talk to us, Anatole! Nobody else cares about us, Anatole!

"Tata Boanda is carrying your mother and sister in his boat. Tata Lekulu is rowing his board with leaves stuffed in his ears while your father lectures him on loving the Lord. Nevertheless, Tata Lekulu is carrying him to safety. Did you know, Mama Mwanza sometimes puts eggs from her own chickens under your hens when you aren't looking? How can you say no one cares about you?" (p. 310)

As Leah cries and understands that she loves this ritually scarred African man, she is calmed and strengthened by his wisdom. As she says to herself, "Anatole's name anchored me to the earth, the water, the skin that held me in like a jar of water." This scene, too, is an embroidery on the travesty of Rachel's being given in marriage to any one of the prospective suitors the Congo can provide. Leah's despair, even mitigated as it is by Anatole's kindness, reflects the dilemma of the adolescent woman. Before her, she has only the aberrant choices Rachel has already experienced; and before both of them, only the model of Orleanna Price and her wistful, naive choice.

BOOK IV:

"What We Lost"

Kingsolver's epigraph for this fourth book comes from the Apochry-pha, those controversial books that Nathan had some fondness for, but that were seldom legitimate parts of any traditional Baptist service. The section's subtitle is "Bel and the Serpent." From the book of that name, 1: 6, the verse reads, "Do you not think that Bel is a living God?/ Do you not see how much he eats and/ drinks every day?" (p. 313) Nathan Price's refrain throughout his African mission has been that of the sin of the worship of false gods (the African) set against reverence for the true Christ. Unrelenting in his objection to any acceptance of Congolese gods, Nathan uses the merged stories of Bel and Daniel, and Daniel and the Serpent, to show Daniel's cunning. There were two separate episodes. The first story is of the Babylonian god, Bel, who daily seemed to devour great quantities of food and drink. (The priests and their families lived off the daily offerings.) Daniel told Cyrus, the Persian ruler, of this trickery; in answer, Cyrus demanded Daniel's life unless he could prove that Bel was not alive. Daniel proceeded to trap the priests by spreading ashes in order to mark the people's footprints as they come to the statue at night. Convinced, Cyrus then puts the seventy priests of Bel to death.

The story of the great serpent, who does live, also proves Daniel's wisdom. Daniel promises Cyrus to kill the snake without using a weapon; he feeds it cakes made of pitch, hair, and fat, and the snake bursts from its gluttony. Because Daniel killed the god as snake, Cyrus responded to the Babylonians' demand that he put his friend in the lions' den for six days. Because Daniel lives and is untouched by the hungry lions, Cyrus comes to believe in God.

While the content of these two stories is here changed to reflect the African context, their use reminds the reader of Nathan's judgmental attitudes, and his admiration for Daniel, about whom he often gives sermons. In effect, Daniel's victories become parables for the way Nathan Price's ministry will also be victorious. In the novel, however, Kingsolver uses the figure of the snake as evil, as killer, as fear-inducing image of the equatorial jungle. The green mamba brings only death. Even though Orleanna has run cobras from her kitchen, the Congolese (like the Americans) fear the snake. And it is Anatole's punishment to find the green mamba in his bedroom upon awakening—in response to his having the community vote about whether or not Leah, a mere woman, could become a hunter.

Barely escaping death, Anatole understands that not only overt political acts are dangerous. But he is so much a part of Leah's life that he cannot avoid encouraging her (he made the bow and arrows for her, taught her to use them, and now hunts with her, even though both the Price family and Anatole himself receive a disproportionately meager share of the meat—more evidence of the community's disapproval). Leah's monologue is both summary and foreshadowing:

"It [the day of the hunt] should have been the most glorious day in our village, but instead it all came crashing down. . . . From the time we first set foot in Kilanga things were going wrong, though we couldn't see it. Even the glorious Independence was not going to be good for everyone, as they'd promised that day on the riverbank, when Lumumba and the Belgians raised up their different promises and the white King lurked somewhere in disguise. There were going to be winners and losers. Now there are wars in the south, killings in the north, rumors that foreigners took over the army and want to murder Lumumba. On the day of the hunt a war was already roaring toward us, whites against blacks. We were all swept up in a greediness we couldn't stop." (p. 352)

Book IV of the novel becomes, then, a less personal section—a weave of white/black, outsider/insider, viewed intimately through the eyes of the villagers, rather than from a historically raced (and therefore much more abstract) perspective. Orleanna's meditation at the start of Book IV, too, is almost entirely political; she extends the Congolese history out fifteen years, twenty-five years, as a means of retrospectively showing the complete ignorance in which she lived in Kilanga.

Through her plot lines, however, Kingsolver forces her reader to keep an eye open for snakes, even as she makes the confrontation between the white and admittedly racist Nathan Price and the village leader, Tata Ndu, more risible. Losing his bid for Rachel, Tata Ndu forces white men's politics down the minister's throat by interrupting one of Nathan's sermons with his call for a community election: the congregation will decide whether or not Jesus is their god by a democratic vote. Amid Nathan's protests, the kitchen election (candidates marked by symbols for the illiterate voters) is held and Jesus loses, 56 to 11. In answer to Nathan's outraged protests, Tata Ndu censures him, in a speech that expresses the essence of postcolonialism:

You believe we are *mwana*, your children, who knew nothing until you came here. Tata Price, I am an old man who learned from other old men. I could tell you the name of the great chief who instructed my father, and all the ones before him, but you would have to know how to sit down and listen. There are one hundred twenty-two. Since the time of our *mankulu* we have made our laws without help from white men. . . . (p. 333)

But even as the reader is prepared by the title and subtitle—what will be the "loss" that demarcates the Price family history? the loss Orleanna has referred to in almost every one of the meditations?—

Kingsolver sweeps back into the political events of the Congolese independence.

When the next threat comes to the Prices, it seems aimed at Nelson, their househelper. It is the chicken house where he sleeps that is targeted. As distant from his family's life as ever, Nathan announces that "this was the unfortunate effect of believing in false idols and he washed his hands of the affair." (p. 357) The family, therefore, has to disobey him in order for Nelson to sleep elsewhere, but they — Daniel-like — make a trap of spread ashes in the chicken house yard.

The next morning, with the ashes revealing several six-toed foot-prints (which identify Tata Ndu, Rachel's suitor and the village witch doctor), the snake planted in Nelson's bed was provoked from the chicken house. As this "basket of death, exploded," (p. 362) in Adah's words, it bit the shoulder of the small Ruth May, whose death was nearly instantaneous.

Kingsolver's last chapter in Book IV is one of stunned mourning for Ruth May, in the midst of the entire village. It also gives Orleanna the power her society and her marriage had kept from her far too long. Orleanna takes charge. She dresses Ruth May for her burial. She brings all the Prices' possessions into the yard and gives them to the neighbors. In her "strange, tireless energy" she has effectively left the house, her marriage, her subordinate role. (p. 372) Kingsolver makes clear that Orleanna says nothing to Nathan; he is no longer any part of her responsibility, nor does she expect him to be of any help (in Leah's memory, "Our father seemed to be nowhere" p. 372). Ironically, as the deranged Nathan returns and insists on baptizing all the black children who come to view Ruth May, and be given the white people's goods, the reader finds that Ruth May herself had never been baptized. Nathan had evidently planned to use her baptism as a part of the aborted ceremony at the river, and since that had not occurred, his conscience about his own child's spiritual safety had gone unaroused.

BOOK V:

"What We Carried Out"

Titled "Exodus," this fifth book focuses on only the women of the Price family—the four that remain, Orleanna, Rachel, Leah and Adah. Its epigraph verse, Exodus 13: 19–22, serves as summary: ". . . And ye shall carry up my bones/ away hence with you./ And they took their journey . . . and encamped . . . / in the edge of the wilderness. . . . / He took not away the pillar of cloud by day, nor the pillar of fire by night." (p. 377) Bereft of all their possessions and their beloved Ruth May, straggling yet purposeful as they walk in the pouring rain, Orleanna and her daughters moved through the equatorial jungle. They walked for days. They existed on a few oranges and some water, a treasured hard-boiled egg, and food from the Congolese who offered them shelter at night. As they headed for Bulungu, where they would be transported to more populated areas, Leah came down with malaria. Carried out of the jungle on a pallet, she stayed with Anatole while Rachel flew off with Axelroot, and Orleanna and Adah bought passage in a truck as they began their journey to the States.

From this point in the novel the disparate narratives are truly separate. Kingsolver's interweaving is no longer necessary, since the four women protagonists are evolving entirely different lives: *home* means something unique for each of them. One of the most interesting elements of the novel's narrative at this point is that readers are made to believe that people who have always lived together, people held together within the confines of a family, could so easily dismiss that family bond and set out alone. Yet Kingsolver convinces the reader that survival dominates their emotional world.

Orleanna, essentially, has long been alone; as the structure of her meditative sections announces, she is trying to become her own person. As she said in the first book, "One has *only* a life of one's own." But to find Leah so ready to jettison her sisters — the reader wonders whether perhaps her devastating illness makes her relinquish them more easily. She herself puzzles over how quickly she gives up her father:

Father was no longer with us. Father and Ruth May both, as simple as that. My mind ached like a broken bone as I struggled to stand in the new place I found myself. I wouldn't see my baby sister again, this I knew. But I hadn't yet considered the loss of my father. I'd walked in his footsteps my whole life, and now without warning my body had fallen in line behind my mother. A woman whose flank and jaw glinted hard as salt when she knelt around a fire with other women; whose pale eyes were fixed on a distance where he couldn't follow. . . . (p. 393)[3]

Leah's willingness to relinquish the male patterns she had been shaping herself into had begun earlier, with her recognition of Nathan's impracticality and his hard-headed insistence on keeping to traditional forms even when circumstances were changing. But she was still somewhat bewildered by her own female gender. The reader assumes here that Leah had learned as much from the way Rachel was being treated as Rachel had herself: the bride price meant nothing when civilization crumbled. A woman was no more than an article of exchange, no matter who had fathered her.

Leah's African life after her family leaves is the weakest part of Kingsolver's novel: there is too much event in the account. Anatole's life is so intertwined with the politics of the Congo that the novel's separation between history and the personal evaporates: what

the reader has is a quick succession of scenes of Leah living alone
while Anatole is imprisoned—at one time in a convent, disguised;
again at Emory University in Atlanta herself, studying; again, living
alone with her children—first one son, then two, finally four—
awaiting news of Anatole's death. Throughout this busy narrative,
Kingsolver shows that Leah's desire to have her own way, and
especially to learn, consistently jeopardizes Anatole's life and fortune in Africa. This woman who has never known her place—
marked visibly by both her whiteness and her gender—does not
relinquish her stubborn needs for any reason.

Leah's choice—to stay in Africa with Anatole, and eventually, to
marry him—is in some ways less of a surprise than is Adah's deci-
sion. Feeling inordinately lucky to leave Africa, she appears at
Emory University and convinces the admissions staff to admit her.
After her undergraduate degree, she goes on to Emory's medical
school. Because Orleanna has chosen to live in Atlanta, fascinated
by both the libraries and the opportunities for activism the city
offers, Adah has not abandoned her mother. Her quest, however, is
entirely separate from any of Orleanna's desires. Adah would never
devote time to social activism because she truly believes, "all animals kill to survive, and we are all animals." (p. 347)

One of the most interesting elements of the post-Africa narrative
is Adah's retraining of her body to "cure" her illnesses. At the
suggestion of a man interning in neurology (who later, once she
was "improved," became her lover), she put herself through a six
month rebirth process. She did not walk; she rolled and crawled
and forced her body to learn to cross-coordinate. As she wryly
notes, "I am losing my slant." (p. 439) She also lost some of the
neurological characteristics she valued—being able to read back-
ward, for one. But in her physical appearance and her strength,
Adah was much closer to normal than she had ever dreamed she
could become.

Ironically, the only daughter who "profits" from living in Africa — in the greedy capitalistic and very colonial sense — is Rachel, the flighty and uncommited oldest child. Perhaps her very lack of social conscience has allowed her to become an opportunist. As she said years before, during their flight from the village in the torrential rains, "The tragedies that happened to Africans were not mine." (p. 367) Rachel always had her eyes open for the main chance. Living with Axelroot and taking his name, though he would never marry her, she did marry the First Attache to Brazzaville, Daniel Du Pree, and finally the older hotel-owner, Remy Fairley. After his death, Rachel owned and managed The Equatorial, the European-style hotel that catered to the colonials who visited, or had stayed in, Africa. Her story, too, continues through the mid-1980s; and Kingsolver gives the reader a 1984 "reunion" of the three sisters — about which Rachel notes "But things fall apart, of course. With us they always do, sooner or later." (p. 483)

The remains of the Price family do little that bonds them as family after these twenty years of separation except continue the story of Nathan Price, at first described as "bearded, wild-haired" (p. 417) and living in the countryside after his house had burned; and then hunted and burned himself, punished for the deaths of children in the crocodile-infested waters. They do, ultimately, bring Orleanna to Africa to visit Ruth May's grave — which cannot be found, nor can the village in which they lived.

Kingsolver throughout the first four books of *The Poisonwood Bible* has shaped her narrative through a well-paced focus on individual scenes — for example, the early calabash-as-globe scene between Leah and Anatole. What occurs in Book V, however, as she brings the daughters' narratives twenty-five years into the future, is that she must omit the scenes she has been constructing: the narrative pace has no room for them.

Structure also changes. Book V is the last of the seven to include Orleanna's meditation as its opening. In that monologue, effective as each of her sections has been, Kingsolver supplies the motive for her quiet withdrawal from life. She cannot grieve enough. In the death of Ruth May, both harmed by Africa and then — in her bur- ial — lost to it, Orleanna has dissolved into little but a mourning soul.

The substance of grief is not imaginary. It's a real as rope or the absence of air, and like both these things it can kill. My body understood there was no safe place for me to be. . . . As long as I kept moving, my grief streamed out behind me like a swimmer's long hair in water. I knew the weight was there but it didn't touch me. Only when I stopped did the sick, dark stuff of it come floating around my face, catching my arms and throat till I began to drown. . . . (p. 381)

In her meditation to Book V, too, Orleanna has become a woman sure of her own sexuality. She has come to understand that the world is divided by gender — men do some kinds of work, women do others, and the bifurcation applies to writing as well. What can a woman writer present as her vision of a complex and difficult world? She moves into this discussion through her defense of her leaving Nathan:

"I didn't set out to leave my husband. Anyone can see I should have, long before, but I never did know how. For women like me, it seems, it's not ours to take charge of beginnings and endings. Not the marriage proposal, the summit conquered, the first shot fired, nor the last one either — the treaty at Appomattox, the knife in the heart. Let men write those stories. I can't. I only know the middle ground where we live our lives. We whistle while Rome burns, or we scrub the floor, depending. . . . *Independence* is a complex word in a foreign tongue. To resist occupation, whether you're a nation or merely a woman, you must understand the language of your enemy. *Conquest* and *liberation* and *democracy* and *divorce* are words that mean squat, basically, when you have hungry children and clothes to get out on the line and it looks like rain." (p. 383)

BOOK VI:

"*Song of the Three Children*";

BOOK VII:

"*The Eyes in the Trees*"

The last two of Kingsolver's seven books are very short; the seventh is an undivided coda, spoken by the spirit of Africa itself, interfused with the soul of Ruth May. Jarring in the quickness with which she brings the novel to its end, some of the detail of Book V — especially the lengthy narrative of Leah and Anatole's lives, focused in the story of the United State's unraveling involvement in Zahir — might more easily have been moved out of the earlier book. While Orleanna's life energy has all but expired, spinning inward to create the vibrant gardens on her quiet island, and Adah's existence as a research physician who specializes in tropical viruses seems to be potently normal, both Rachel and Leah take the narrative in new directions. Rachel becomes the opportunistic colonizer who profits from servicing the wealthy white population; Leah almost becomes Africa itself — pained, poor, valuing her sons for the variations in their skin colors, and continuing in her own whiteness to imperil not only her husband but now her sons. In her zeal to become African, Leah has never accepted her difference.

Moving from Orleanna's comments in her last meditation, the reader sees that the choices Kingsolver has made here at the end of *The Poisonwood Bible* are her considered choices as the woman writer she is. With Book VI, she slips away from the carefully constructed format of the first five books. Orleanna, like Nathan, is missing from the narrative. What remains is the story of the three surviving daughters, and the book's title, "Song of the Three Children," is the same as the verse from *The Apocrypha* that stands as epigraph. The key words there are "justice" and "deliver us." [4]

The three valedictory sections that follow are spoken by Rachel, Leah, and Adah. While Rachel's section is predictable, she has a healthy awareness of what a white person's being in Africa entails. In her consistent vernacular, "From the very first moment I set foot in the Congo, I could see we were not in charge. . . . Father's mistake, see, was to try to convert the whole entire shebang over into just his exact way of thinking."(p. 517). Forgiving of the comedy in Rachel's diction, Kingsolver turns to more serious matters in the latter two sections. Leah's centers on race, and she concludes with the self-revealing comment that "I wake up in love, and work my skin to darkness under the equatorial sun. I look at my four boys, who are the colors of silt, loam, dust, and clay, an infinite palette for children of their own, and I understand that time erases whiteness altogether." (p. 526) But it is for Adah — the least romantic of the three — to write the commemoration for her father, "a man who believed he could tell nothing but the truth," she concludes, "while he set down for all time the Poisonwood Bible." (p. 533)

Just as Kingsolver moved from the traditional Bible for the source of her first books' epigraphs, and then drew from The Apocrapha — in deference to Nathan's law-breaking propensities, by the time of Book VII, there is no epigraph at all. The function of art is to break through formal constraints; the greatest novels shatter prescriptive form. Her choices within Book VII, "The Eyes in the Trees," may be less effective than she has hoped, however, because the clarity of form in Books I through VI is helpful to readers. Suddenly, there is no epigraph at all, no meditation (though Orleanna appears, but as the cared for, not the caregiver), and no named narrative sections. There is, instead, the unnamed speaker of Book VII:

The glide of belly on branch. The mouth thrown open wide, sky blue. I am all that is here. The eyes in the trees never blink. You plead with me your daughter sister sister for release, but I am no little beast and have no reason to judge. . . . (p. 537)

The concluding section offers information along with its metaphor; its chief event is the visit of Orleanna, Rachel, Leah, and Adah to what was the location of their remote village. Now disappeared from both geography and memory, the village resonates through the country they are able to visit. It has its crystallizing moment in the village market, when a Congolese woman sells the Price party some of her carvings, three ebony elephants for the grandsons and, for Orleanna, "a gift: the tiny wooden okapi, perfectly carved." (p. 541) Full circle, a totem for the bereft mother to take back to her own isolated paradise, her island garden, the representation of the initial okapi she had first glimpsed on the shore of the river that proved to be so treacherous, yet so seminal for her and her family. One of the closing images of the novel is this, "Orleanna pockets her small miracle, as she has done for the whole of her life." (p. 542)

In the last paragraph of the coda, Kingsolver relieves Orleanna of her grief. Words from the spirit of Africa cum Ruth May erase the weight of memory that has been the mother's to carry for these twenty-odd years. Like a benizon, the unidentified voice urges Orleanna on:

Listen. Slide the weight from your shoulders and move forward. You are afraid you might forget, but you never will. You will forgive and remember. Think of the vine that curls from the small square plot that was once my heart. That is the only marker you need. Move on. Walk forward into the light. (p. 543)

3

The Novel's Reception

$\mathbf{T}$*he Poisonwood Bible* has become an important novel over the several years since its publication in autumn of 1998. As Kingsolver's fourth novel, it was widely reviewed: few American women writers had built such wide — and stable — readership. But *Poisonwood Bible* differed in many respects from Kingsolver's first three best-sellers, and it does not seem strange that many of its best reviews came out during 1999 — as if the act of reading and judging such a large book took time in itself. *The Bean Trees* and *Pigs in Heaven* were narratives about the young resourceful woman character become instant mother, and her contradictory attitudes toward the Native American tribe that was her child's true home. *Animal Dreams* again presented a college educated woman who had completed medical school, and her more adventurous sister, this time caught in a cultural surround they both denied and hungered for. All Kingsolver's earlier novels had been set in the Southwestern United States; all had comparatively straightforward, even simple, plots. All had a woman protagonist that, without too much of a stretch, could be identified with some aspects of the novelist herself.

Although Kingsolver had published poems and short stories, and had worked as a journalist, the consistently positive reviews of *The Bean Trees* were unexpected. First novels rarely sell at all; *The Bean Trees* eventually sold well over a million copies, an almost unheard of record for a serious novel, and was translated into many other languages. Much to the author's surprise, the Kingsolver phenomenon had begun. As Margaret Randall wrote in her review in *The Women's Review of Books, The Bean Trees* is "a first novel that's fast reading but long staying."[1] She describes its first effect as "light" and "delicious," but then emphasizes that — for all Kingsolver's comic tone and effective use of vernacular language — the novel "is addressing and connecting two of our most important issues." Randall sees these to be "invasion. . . . the sexual invasion of a child's body and the political invasion of a nation's sovereignty." The novel, however, does no political posturing; instead — and this is Kingsolver's gift — the book tells "the story of ordinary people who understand both realities [of invasion] as they touch their own . . . a story about racism, sexism and dignity."[2]

Difficult to define (in a later section Randall calls the book "one of those old-fashioned stories"), *The Bean Trees* charmed readers into seeing the real in its positive dimensions. Two years later, *Animal Dreams* — despite its more elaborate narrative structure — did the same. Here the political streams are more obvious: Hallie is, in fact, living and working in Nicaragua. She is the sister who went to war, while Codi, the drop-out from medical practice, went home to Grace, Arizona. But in the poverty-bound mining territory to which she returns, the politics of wage slavery and unionization grows to dominate her story. Paul Gray — admiringly — calls this an "eco-feminist" book;[3] Jane Smiley also places it in the company of other serious novels by writers working hard to avoid the apocalyptic: Kingsolver is, rather, "trying to rewrite the political, cultural, and spiritual relationships between our country's private and public spheres."[4] That she does so by concentrating on particularities instead of a more abstracted canvas is why she is a novelist.

It took only this second novel (and the interest in the collection of her short stories—*Homeland and Other Stories*, published in 1989) to move Kingsolver into the "serious author" category. She had been taken out of the class of the writer who could write one good novel and then was heard from no more; Lisa See's profile in *Publishers Weekly* signaled that change of status. Having published *The Bean Trees* in 1988, *Homeland* in 1989, and *Animal Dreams* in 1990 was an important strategy: readers were not able to forget who Barbara Kingsolver was. Sales of *Animal Dreams* were almost as strong as those of *The Bean Trees*.

See's profile states that *Animal Dreams* draws in "all of [Kingsolver's] previous themes—Native Americans, U.S. involvement in Nicaragua, environmental issues, parental relationships, women's taking charge of their own lives" and then describes Kingsolver as this committed, almost visionary, writer.[5] She quotes the author: " 'Those issues will keep turning up in everything I write. They are central to my reason for living. The only authentic and moving fiction you can write is about the things that are most urgent to you and worth disturbing the universe over.' "[6]

One emphasis that dominated reviews of Kingsolver's third novel, *Pigs in Heaven*, the 1993 continuation of the story of the Cherokee child Turtle, the adopted daughter from *The Bean Trees*, was that of Kingsolver's training as biologist. Trying to position her as scientific observer rather than as what she appeared to be, a modern woman with a talent for creating believable voice and story, the latter perhaps autobiographical, was one way of sidestepping the all too common argument that women writers wrote realistically for their intended readers, who were most often women book buyers, and therefore were probably guilty of sentimentalizing life.

It is also likely that the emphasis on Kingsolver as scientist was a way of deflecting attention from the fact that in this second novel about the Cherokee child the author had complicated the narrative problem of where Turtle belonged. In *The Bean Trees*, Taylor, the adoptive mother, used duplicity that smacked of racist manipulation in order to adopt the child; here when the Cherokee nation demands the return of its child, mother and daughter run. For a novelist acclaimed as one with a moral conscience, these two novels posed difficulties. Laura Shapiro writes that Kingsolver here "takes a risk she hasn't taken before: she challenges her own strong, '60s-style politics by pitting its cultural correctness against the boundless love between mother and child." Yet, Shapiro continues, rather than being a polemic, *Pigs in Heaven* is "a complex drama in which heroes and villains play each other's parts—and learn from them."[7] Karen Karbo's review in *The New York Times Book Review* had made the same point, that Kingsolver "manages to maintain her political views without sacrificing the complexity of her characters' predicaments."[8]

In the world of writing by women authors, if one likely charge is sentimentalizing (a label hard to avoid when the plot hinges on a mother-daughter relationship), the other easy target is that much fiction by women is "issues oriented," and may be more sociology than literature. That Kingsolver from the start was writing about the abuse of children, single parenthood, land waste, water pollution, ethnic difference and poverty surely gave her readers ample reason to say that she wrote "problem" fiction. Few readers have done so, however; and even few reviewers have. Her own statements about her fiction's themes do place her squarely in such a category. On the difference between the Native American view of community and that of mainstream United States culture, Kingsolver writes, "The media view the basic unit of good as what is best for the child; the tribe sees it as what is best for the group. These are two very different value systems with no point of intersection."[9]

She speaks too about the materialistic ways of evaluating cultures, especially since the Native American life is often one of poverty: "It has to do with our mythology in this country that if you are smart enough and work hard enough, you will make it. It allows us to perpetuate this huge gulf between the well-off and the desperately poor. . . . poverty is viewed as shameful. In this culture, it's more honorable to steal than to beg."[10]

Although it took five years of work, Kingsolver's *The Poisonwood Bible*, in many ways, extended and relocated the same set of themes — ethnic difference, underscored by starkly different concepts of both individual success and community. In retrospect, it seems as if the many reviews of her earlier novels were already preparing readers for what might have appeared to be a very different kind of book.

Reviewed in every possible medium in the autumn of 1998, *The Poisonwood Bible* has been nearly always praised. Surely a political work, and surely a feminized story — in that the narrators were all women (the mother and her four daughters) — Kingsolver escaped the charges that might have been expected — the almost stereotyped commentary on the U.S. involvement with the Congolese struggle, the almost too harsh criticism of American missionary efforts to change the beliefs of an African people.

Publishers Weekly did call the novel "risky," in fact, in its August, 1998, advance review — "risky but resoundingly successful." To move her fiction out of the American Southwest, which she portrayed with such authority, and take on Africa was to force herself to grow as a writer. For this unnamed reviewer, Kingsolver "moves into new moral terrain in this powerful, convincing and emotionally resonant novel." *Publishers Weekly* saw the book as "a compelling family saga," filled with much "trenchant character portrayal."[11] Donna Seaman in the *Booklist* advance review was less impressed with the Price family narrators than she was with the scope of the book as a whole: "no facet of civilization or the human spirit goes unexplored in this measureless saga of hubris and deliverance."[12]

A novel of 546 pages seemed to elicit sweeping comments. It was often referred to as a saga or an epic, often compared with Joseph Conrad's *Heart of Darkness*, and often praised for leaving the author's customary myopic view of the United States to scan a wider arena. Yet as Verlyn Klinkenborg notes in his *New York Times Book Review* essay,

The Congo permeates "The Poisonwood Bible," and yet this is a novel that is just as much about America, a portrait, in absentia, of the nation that sent the Prices to save the souls of a people for whom it felt only contempt. . . . The Congolese are not savages who need saving . . . and there is nothing passive in their tolerance of missionaries.[13]

The Klinkenborg review brings out two other important facets of *The Poisonwood Bible*. One is the fact that Kingsolver's choosing Orleanna and the daughters to tell the story only more firmly imbeds for the reader the location of real power, which resides in the father.

Nathan Price narrates nothing. And yet his certitude — and the literal-minded ferocity with which he expresses it — is the altar around which these women arrange themselves. We already know his story, Kingsolver implies. Most of what we have always heard, she suggests, are stories told by men like him.[14]

The reviewer is correct, too, in seeing that Kingsolver's Congo is *not* Conrad's. It may appear to be dim and brutal but what the women characters (except for Rachel) come to realize is "the near-perfect adaptation of the Congolese to the harsh conditions of their existence, a fittedness that is beautiful in itself. With that knowledge comes the discovery of the Prices' own profound ignorance."[15] In this important sense, then, Kingsolver has attempted to recuperate the dark continent, and by peopling it with distinctive — if necessarily minor — characters has managed to humanize it in a remarkable way.

Among the reviews that did nothing but praise *The Poisonwood Bible* is one by Gayle Greene, who makes the venerating move to compare the Kingsolver novel to Toni Morrison's *Beloved*. Emphasizing the way the writing works, Greene calls *Bible* "a complex, textured work, its imagery patterns resonating across levels of meaning. The idea of feeding, for example, plays out on ecological, biological, psychological, and political levels: ants eat their way across Africa, the forest eats itself yet lives forever, crocodiles devour children; there is famine, hunting, poison, a snake in the belly, a dog-eat-dog world, a consumer society, a stewpot we're all in together. It is multivocal and multiphonic, its meaning not in a single voice but in the play of voices against one another, the mother and four daughters who tell this tale making five tones like those of the ancient pentatonic scale."[16]

John Leonard's *Nation* review is the kind of response an author might be tempted to frame, and hang modestly in a place where only she could see it. Replete with comparisons to Conrad, Graham Greene, Evelyn Waugh and Hemingway, as a means of contrast, Leonard adds Doris Lessing and Nadine Gordimer to the writers Kingsolver might now join. He sees the book as belonging to the "remarkable" Price women, and finds the story to be about mothers "white American and black Congolese and matriarchal Africa herself." The plot returns again and again — whether metaphorically or literally — to the child lost. With what Leonard calls her "matrohistorical scale of justice," he claims that Kingsolver "has gone back to Africa and somehow transfigured it."

His highest praise is for Kingsolver's narrative structure:

As in the keyed chords of a Baroque sonata, movements of the personal, the political, the historical and even the biological contrast and correspond. As in a Bach cantata, the choral stanza, the recitatives and the da capo arias harmonize. . . . [17]

Perhaps it was for the British reviewers of this novel to lend a little acerbity to the uniform American praise. Dealing with colonial and postcolonial matters strikes the English reviewers as less innovative, for one thing; and their understanding of what happened in the Congo during the 1960s was less often obscured by the sloganized "I like Ike" charade of United States political coverup. When Carol Birch gives *The Poisonwood Bible* a favorable review, she does so because of the "rounded, convincing portraits" in this "brilliantly realised epic." She warns the prospective reader, however, that Kingsolver tends toward the didactic; in fact, the otherwise good novel is spoiled by what Birch calls the "great swathes of polemic" in its last quarter. She advises the reader to enjoy "the sheer power of the story . . . [concluding] Kingsolver is a great storyteller but she is no philosopher and has a shaky grip on moral relativism."[18]

For Isobel Montgomery, who points out that Kingsolver has included at the back of the novel "a bibliography that names all the usual suspects," the fact that the story is nothing new matters less than the way the author tells the story: the book "is redeemed from cliche by the way Kingsolver embraces her prefab narrative structure and tells an old story from a new perspective."[19]

By the time of the paperback issue in January of 2000, however, even the British reviewer Nicholas Lezard has become a believer;

he sees that *The Poisonwood Bible* is "a good book" precisely because it is not "a mixture of magic realism and patronisingly soulful rebuke of whitey." Rather, the book "both learns and teaches us the patterns of life in an isolated rain-forest village, or in a shanty town; it helps you make sense of poverty, and through literary technique, rather than bald exposition or a rant."[20]

That *The Poisonwood Bible* won nearly every possible fiction prize — except the Pulitzer and the PEN/Faulkner, for both of which it was runner-up — reified the many positive reviews, not to mention the book's sales. (It was not until some months after its publication that it was chosen to be an Oprah's Book selection, so momentum continued to build.)

The Poisonwood Bible did win the ABBY (the American Booksellers Book of the Year, an award for which Kingsolver's other three novels had also been nominated). It did win the Patterson Fiction Prize from the Poetry Center, and was short-listed for Great Britain's Orange Prize. It was one of the *New York Times* "Ten Best Books of 1998" and the *Los Angeles Times* and the *Village Voice* "Best Books for 1998." It appeared on the Canadian North 49 "Valuable Picks" list and on the New York Public Library "25 Books to Remember" list.[21]

Praise from a different sort of critic might bring this section to an interesting close. In the "Bookshelf" section of *O*, Oprah's magazine appeared Hillary Clinton's reasons for admiring *The Poisonwood Bible*. Mrs. Clinton wrote that the novel was "one of the most powerful books I've read about the evil consequences of patriarchal oppression, be it personal, cultural or political. The story is movingly told through the voices of four sisters and their mother. It reminded me that every woman faces unique challenges and choices, and that all too often women find themselves trapped by their circumstances."[22]

4

The Novel's Performance

A selection of the influential Oprah Winfrey television program's book club, Kingsolver's 1998 novel continues to maintain momentum. Even though *Prodigal Summer*, her most recent novel, was published in autumn of 2000 and quickly made its way onto the *New York Times* Best-seller list, the novel being read throughout the States and abroad is *The Poisonwood Bible*, now available in the cheaper paperback edition.

The reception of *Prodigal Summer*, in fact, may be comparatively cool because many readers expected Kingsolver to continue on from the level of excellence she had achieved in *The Poisonwood Bible*. *Prodigal Summer*, with its tripartite story line and its tendency to voice a didactic ecological conservationism, has been something of a disappointment. As Jennifer Schuessler said in her review of the novel in the November 5 *New York Times Book Review*, "Kingsolver is an ambitious writer, but here she has bitten off a lot that she doesn't really chew."[1] For Schuessler, the comparison to *The Poisonwood Bible* seems necessary:

[there] the interlocking first-person narratives of the crazed evangelist's wife and four daughters provided glimpses of dangerous, unmasterable reality through the cracks between the characters' incomplete visions.

She laments that *Prodigal Summer* does not have "the emotional intensity and wide-angle vision of . . . Kingsolver's magnificent 1998 epic about a self-destructing missionary family in the newly independent Congo."[2]

Kingsolver herself recognized that *The Poisonwood Bible* was her most serious, and most ambitious, fiction yet. She explained its subject candidly: "This story came from passion, culpability, anger and a long-term fascination with Africa, and my belief that what happened to the Congo is one of the most important political parables of our century. I've been thinking about this story for as long as I've had eyes and a heart."[3] She does not shrink from using the term "postcolonial" in reference to it.

I live in a society that grew prosperous from exploiting others. England has a strong tradition of postcolonial literature but here in the U.S., we can hardly even say the word "postcolonial." We like to think we're the good guys. So we persist in our denial, and live with a legacy of exploitation and racial arrogance that continues to tear people apart, in a million large and small ways. As long as I have been a writer I've wanted to address this, to try to find a way to own our terrible history honestly and construct some kind of redemption. It's a preposterously outsized ambition. . . . [4]

Taking the task, and the labels, on her shoulders, Kingsolver writes *The Poisonwood Bible*, acknowledging that the historical politics was its very scaffold. "We didn't make the awful decisions our government imposed on Africa. We didn't call for the assassination of Lumumba; we hardly even knew about it. We just inherited these decisions, and now have to reconcile them with our sense of who we are. We're the captive witnesses, just like the wife and daughters of Nathan Price. Male or female, we are not like him. *That* is what I wanted to write about."[5]

Her purpose in conceptualizing the narrative, then, was bound to lead to some reader's negative reactions to the book. Perhaps the treatment of the political theme in the last sections of the book (so that the inclusion of politics became less than seamless) triggered the objections that were voiced. The slim Book VII, for example, includes a two paragraph passage (only four pages from the end of the novel) describing the death of Mobutu, the long-term Congolese ruler. Although Kingsolver links his corrupt rule with the title of Book VII, his appearance — and demise — feel extraneous to the story of the four Price women as they return to Africa. The Mobutu story begins mid-paragraph, in fact:

A good boil, they say here, a good boil purifies the rotten meat. After thirty-five years the man Mobutu has run away in the night. Thirty-five years of sleep like death, and now the murdered land draws a breath, moves its fingers, takes up life through its rivers and forests. The eyes in the trees are watching.[6]

In tandem with the occasional protest over the overt political stance the novel comes to assume are the questions readers have about the character of Nathan Price. Kingsolver refuses to type Nathan as a male or an evil character. He is, rather, "a character, invented by me, for no other purpose than to serve my plot. . . . Nathan is single-minded all right, but hardly one-sided. He's ferocious and cowardly; charismatic and revolting; brilliant and tedious." She points out that he does not stand for the entire ministerial profession, but rather that he is "a symbolic figure [since] *The Poisonwood Bible* is a political allegory, suggesting many things about the way the U.S. and Europe have approached Africa with a history of cultural arrogance and misunderstanding at every turn."[7]

What happens when she begins to work out a plan for a novel, Kingsolver admits, is that she is starting with an idea, a theme. She finds (largely, by creating) characters that will enable her to flesh out the theme. Somewhat scientific in her methods, she begins with the "meaning" and works toward an interesting set of stories — and characters — that will bring the theme to her readers; she says that she aims to "write my way to an answer."[8] One key to capturing reader interest is a narrative packed with details; in fact, she says "A novel is a rich collection of details all added together in a way that satisfactorily answers some of life's universal questions." The tenacity to learn to know the details, the facts of the places and people of every fiction, makes the good novelist into a better one, as Kingsolver says in her 1998 review of Cathleen Schine's *The Evolution of Jane.*[9]

Beyond the conventional wisdom about writing fiction (i.e., that one creates characters and does not work from real people; that one tries to find a language and a structure germane to the work being written), Kingsolver insists that the craft of fiction must move beyond aesthetics. As she says in an interview with David Gergen, "We need new stories." She refers to the former myths of American culture, that of Horatio Alger and what she calls "sort of national religion . . . about the glory and the power of the individual and our great unifying myths . . . that anybody can make it in this country if he's smart enough and ambitious enough." It's an unfair belief "because the other side of that story is that if you're not making it, you must be either stupid or lazy. So a lot of self-blame goes along with poverty. It's very isolating."[10]

In answer to Gergen's questions about certain of her novels, she concludes that the answer is people creating community: "everything I write is about the idea of community and about the special challenge in the United States of balancing our idealization of the individual, our glorification of, of personal freedom and the individual with the importance of community, how to balance those two offices."[11]

Much of the published material on Kingsolver as writer deals with her first three novels, her collection of stories, her book about the copper mine strike, and her published essays: the emphasis by interviewers and critics alike was in rescuing her, to some extent, from the ghetto of her being a best-selling woman novelist whose work would never be taught in United States college classrooms. Too much focused on the domestic scene, on women's lives lived in generally tight financial circumstances, on the themes of a mother's concern for her child and her need for community to buttress her own abilities to rear that child — Kingsolver's first books read as if a nineteenth century writer had awakened to the hard facts of the mechanized, slightly inhumanized twentieth century.

One of the reasons her customary readers, and a bevy of new ones, found *The Poisonwood Bible* to be so dramatically different — and so clearly praiseworthy — was that it seemed to avoid the intimate domestic novel scenario. At first glance, Africa was not Arizona (or Kentucky or Appalachia); the primary characters were men — Nathan Price and the various leaders of the African villages; and the struggle was far beyond finding rent money or repairing a car so it would get its owner to work yet another month. But of course, ultimately, Kingsolver was writing about the domestic (even though the cultural purview had changed), the relationship among family members, and the need for community. Even the overt political theme was tied, perhaps unnecessarily, into the family dynamic: both Patrice Lumumba and Ruth May Price died on January 17, 1961. Whenever Leah mourned her baby sister, Anatole mourned Lumumba; ironically, the respective "importance" of the commemoration of these death days caused friction within their family unit.

There is another such coincidence, one that somewhat detracts from the serious thrust of the novel. One of the rumors that live past Nathan Price's death (i.e., execution) is that he had five wives (which would have made him a very wealthy and respected man, even if a white man), but that they all left him. Taken as part of the Price lore, his daughters thought little of the story until it dawned on them — they, Orleanna and the four of them, were his "five wives."[12] The women who cared for him, who submitted their lives to maintaining his position, were cast in the role of "wife," regardless of their familial relationship. In the myth of the Congo, none of them exists except Nathan. Their situation is as colonial, and as subject to the patriarchy, as Africa's itself.

To reinforce her belief that all fiction must have thematic importance, Kingsolver in the late 1990s created a literary prize for the best political fiction of a two year period, a prize which she funds from her writing income. The Bellwether Award, to be given biennially, consists of a monetary prize of $25,000, along with a publishing contract for the winning manuscript. In the year 2001, Donna M. Gershten's *Kissing the Virgin's Mouth*, the first of the Bellwether novels, will appear from HarperCollins. More than 120 manuscripts were submitted for that period's contest, judged by writers Grace Paley and Ruth Ozeki. In Kingsolver's praise for Gershten's book she said it was "a beautifully written, lyrical novel that carries exactly the kind of political boldness and complexity that we are hoping to promote with this prize. Its heroine is irresistible for her smart sexiness, her moral complexities, and her refusal to be a victim as she constructs her own ideology of female survival against the tyrannies of her culture. This writer has a stunning talent for shifting a reader's vision of the world. I really believe it sets a standard for what we're defining as a literature of social responsibility."[13]

Kingsolver's phrase, "a literature of social responsibility," seems an apt description of all her novels, but most expressly of *The Poisonwood Bible*.

5

Further Reading and Discussion Questions

(1) Any discussion of the works of Barbara Kingsolver must take some notice of the facts that this is a writer who is comparatively untrained in the business of writing. Most authors in the United States have majored in English and done graduate work—usually in Masters of Fine Arts programs in one of the established MFA programs in the country or in doctoral programs in literature. In Kingsolver's case, both her undergraduate degree and her graduate work were taken in scientific fields. As a practicing writer, she was as frequently writing scientific essays and grant proposals as she was journalism. Does her fiction reveal any impact of her study of biology, anthropology, and evolutionary biology?

(2) A great amount of energy in United States publishing and marketing is spent categorizing a book and its author. Obviously, Kingsolver would first be identified as a woman writer; then as a contemporary writer (one well under forty when her first novel appeared); then as an American writer, and a Southwestern one, since much of her early fiction dealt with Arizona; then perhaps as a Southern writer, as her roots and interest in Appalachia became more visible; then perhaps as a proponent of ecological conserva-

tion. She would also be identified with heterosexual practices, with mothering, with a fascination with community and its building, and with spirituality. As a white, educated woman, the daughter of a medical doctor and a well-educated mother, Kingsolver also has had advantages in her life that make her — despite the themes in her fiction — a privileged writer.

If you were the publisher for her next novel, how would you market Barbara Kingsolver? Which of these descriptions would you emphasize? Which are more relevant to *The Poisonwood Bible*?

(3) Meredith Sue Willis talks about the way Kingsolver draws Appalachian characters, but the critic is more impressed with the way the author sets her characters in motion, drawing on what she calls "the fine old propensity for *moving on.*. . . . [the] powerful mountain tradition of emigration. The reasons are many, not always happy. In the 18th century, the North Britons who settled the American backcountry were above all people on the move — as individuals, as families, sometimes as whole clans."[1] Even in *The Poisonwood Bible*, where it may be least crucial, does Kingsolver create characters who seem poised to take up the search, if not the quest?

(4) Critic Maureen Ryan, in a 1995 essay, attempted to come to some reasons for Kingsolver's immense popularity, and concluded that it may be "because it is the exemplary fiction for our age: aggressively politically correct, yet fundamentally conservative."[2] She contextualizes her remark by continuing, it's a fiction that is not minimalist or shocking; it is rather "traditional realistic fiction," with a definite emphasis on the morality of the characters' lives and acts. Do you agree with this assessment of Kingsolver's novels, particularly *The Poisonwood Bible*?

(5) Although the interest in home and a person's placement there is not strictly speaking "conservative," the point of Roberta Rubenstein's essay on Kingsolver is that frequently a character's

"return home" is the quest of the fiction.[3] She points to the fact that a man's pride—as Doc Homer in *Animal Dreams*, and we might add Nathan Price in *The Poisonwood Bible*—often interferes with the fulfillment of any return home. Does the fact that at least some of the characters in *The Poisonwood Bible* return to the southern United States make this critical observation valid? How would you describe the "quest" of the sisters who remain in Africa, Rachel and Leah?

(6) Charlotte M. Wright takes on these arguments that Kingsolver is conservative in her emphasis that "The literary territory Barbara Kingsolver continues to mine—in her fiction, her nonfiction, and her poetry—is a multicultural, political, and passionate place."[4] How does the author's interest in the non-white (i.e., the multicultural) shape her writing?

(7) Wright also defends the fact that Kingsolver's books sell so well: they are "by no means simplistic. There are no easy answers for the world's problems; there are lots of complex questions."[5] Can you defend the complex structure of *The Poisonwood Bible* on the grounds that its multiple narrative lines, and multiple narrators, are necessary to capture the fact of "no easy answers"?

(8) Kingsolver herself, in a recent addition to the "Dialogue" section of the Barbara Kingsolver website, speaks to the structure of the 1998 novel. "The book is a political allegory, in which the small incidents of characters' lives shed light on larger events in our world. The Prices carry into Africa a whole collection of beliefs about religion, technology, health, politics, and agriculture, just as industrialized nations have often carried these beliefs into the developing world in an extremely arrogant way, very certain of being right (even to the point of destroying local ideas, religion and leadership), even when it turns out—as it does in this novel—that those attitudes are useless, offensive or inapplicable." Which of the Prices would this description fit? Which members of the family evince attitudes

which seem "useless, offensive or inapplicable"? How do the other family members try to salvage their efforts from the destruction that would ordinarily await them?

(9) Kingsolver makes reference in her novel to the title of Chinua Achebe's famous, and influential, novel of stifled African independence, *Things Fall Apart*, originally published in 1959. In Achebe's book, the strong but misguided African, Okonkwo, succumbs to the sin of pride and is punished by his countrymen. Exiled for seven years, his return is marred by the presence of powerful white missionaries. Eventually he commits suicide, rather than be seen as weak. The whites do not understand his act. With Achebe's focus on the African pride, and African culture as inviolable by the whites, how does *Things Fall Apart* contrast with Kingsolver's *The Poisonwood Bible*?

(10) Kingsolver has often commented that among her favorite authors are Doris Lessing, William Faulkner, Eudora Welty, and John Steinbeck. Of the latter, she recently wrote that it is Steinbeck's ability to speak for the multi-racial character, and the woman character, that she admires. Do you find qualities and techniques in *The Poisonwood Bible* that remind you of the work of any of these other American writers?

(11) Kingsolver has been attacked for her portrait of the Christian missionary, Nathan Price. Some readers have found *The Poisonwood Bible* anti-religious. To that charge, she has said that "I'm only opposed to arrogant proselytizing. Nathan Price is, indeed, an arrogant proselytizer, but he's not the only agent of Christianity here. His wife and daughters take different paths toward more open-minded kinds of spirituality, and I called in Brother Fowles specifically to represent Christian mission in a kinder voice. . . . my favorite character is Brother Fowles, whose role in the novel is to redeem both Christianity and the notion of mission. I happen to think religion is a wonderful thing."[6] Given the fact that few critics

have ever commented on Brother Fowles, or the sacrificed parrot he leaves behind, is Kingsolver's apologia convincing? If the positive depiction of the Christian occurs chiefly in a very minor character, might she need to re-structure her novel?

(12) Kingsolver reports that every one of the daughters has been championed by some groups of readers. Does this surprise you? Which of the four might be less a favorite than others? Why?

(13) She also notes that the character of Orleanna has been divisive: some readers find her behavior—as wife and also as mother—questionable, if not lax and indefensible. How does Orleanna strike you as reader? Does your opinion of her change in different parts of the novel? What does Kingsolver lose by having her voice appear, for the most part, in a retrospective narrative? What does she gain?

Notes

1. The Novelist

1. Biographical material throughout this section is drawn from Kingsolver's essay to her mother (in *I've Always Meant to Tell You: Letters to Our Mothers/ An Anthology of Contemporary Women Writers*, ed. Constance Warloe [New York: Pocket Books, Simon & Schuster, 1997], pp. 248–61; "Interview with Barbara Kingsolver," *Backtalk: Women Writers Speak Out*, ed. Donna Perry (New Brunswick, New Jersey: Rutgers University Press, 1993), pp. 143–69; the Annenberg/CPB film on Barbara Kingsolver for *Signature: Contemporary Southern Writers*, 1997; and Kingsolver's informative web site: *www.kingsolver.com*.

2. Barbara Kingsolver, *I've Always Meant to Tell You*, pp. 251–52.

3. Ibid., p. 253.

4. "Interview with Barbara Kingsolver," *Backtalk*, p. 149.

5. Ibid., pp. 147–148.

6. Kingsolver film, *Signature*, 1997.

7. Ibid.

8. Barbara Kingsolver, *I've Always Meant to Tell You*, pp. 255–56.

9. Kingsolver film, *Signature*, 1997.

10. Barbara Kingsolver, "Introduction to the 1996 Printing" of *Holding the Line* (Ithaca, New York: Cornell University Press, 1989, 1996), p. xi.

11. Kingsolver film, *Signature*, 1997.

12. Ibid.

13. "Interview with Barbara Kingsolver," *Backtalk*, p. 150.

14. Kingsolver film, *Signature*, 1997.

15. Ibid.

16. Ibid.

17. "Interview with Barbara Kingsolver," *Backtalk*, p. 158.

18. Ibid.

19. Ibid.

20. Quoted in Lisa See, "Barbara Kingsolver," *Publishers Weekly*, Vol 237, no. 35 (August 31, 1990), p. 47.

21. "Interview with Barbara Kingsolver," *Backtalk*, p. 162.

22. Sarah Kerr, "The Novel as Indictment," *New York Times Magazine* (October 11, 1998), p. 52.

23. Barbara Kingsolver, "Dialogue" section of Kingsolver Web material.

24. Ibid.

25. Ibid.

2. The Novel

1. Barbara Kingsolver, *The Poisonwood Bible* (New York: Harper-Collins, 1998), p. 80; all subsequent references are to this edition and are in parentheses.

2. Carolyn Marvin and David W. Ingle, *Blood Sacrifice and the Nation: Totem Rituals and the American Flag* (New York: Columbia University Press, 1999), p. 205.

3. As Leah had commented earlier, "But where is the place for girls in that kingdom? The rules don't quite apply to us, nor protect us either. . . ." (244)

4. To turn to the "Song of the Three Holy Children" as it is included in the book of Daniel, three men—Shadrach, Meshack, and Abednego—are cast into the fiery furnace. The heating of the furnace destroys the Chaldaeans, and when an angel appears, the flames are changed to wind. The hymn concludes with a thanksgiving; the three men are themselves

saved. *The Poisonwood Bible* too ends with at least a limited thanksgiving: three of the four children have survived.

3. The Novel's Reception

1. Margaret Randall, "Human Comedy," *Women's Review of Books* 5, no. 8 (May 1988), p. 1.

2. Ibid., p. 3; see also Carolyn See (who calls the novel "the work of a visionary"), *Los Angeles Times Book Review*, (March 12, 1989), p. 14.

3. Paul Gray, "Call of the Eco-Feminist," *Time* (September 24, 1990), p. 87.

4. Jane Smiley, "In One Small Town, the Weight of the World," *New York Times Book Review*, (September 2, 1990), p. 2.

5. Lisa See, "Barbara Kingsolver," *Publishers Weekly* 237, no. 35 (August 31, 1990), p. 46.

6. Kingsolver as quoted in See, ibid., p. 47.

7. Laura Shapiro, "A Novel Full of Miracles," *Newsweek* (July 12, 1993), p. 61.

8. Karen Karbo, "And Baby Makes Two," *New York Times Book Review* (June 27, 1993), p. 9.

9. Quoted in Lynn Karpen's interview, "The Role of Poverty," *New York Times Book Review* (June 27, 1992), p. 9.

10. Ibid.

11. "The Poisonwood Bible," *Publishers Weekly* (August 10, 1998), p. 366.

12. Donna Seaman, "The Poisonwood Bible," *Booklist* (August 1998), p. 1922.

13. Verlyn Klinkenborg, "Going Native," *New York Times Book Review* (October 18, 1998), p. 7.

14. Ibid.

15. Ibid.

16. Gayle Greene, "Independence Struggle," *Women's Review of Books* 16, no. 7 (April 1999).

17. John Leonard, "Kingsolver in the Jungle, Catullus & Wolfe at the Door," *Nation* 268, no. 2 (January 11–18, 1999), p. 28.

18. Carol Birch, "The Missionary Imposition," *The Independent* (London), (February 6, 1999), "Features," p. 14.

19. Isobel Montgomery, "Mission Impossible," *The Guardian* (London), (February 13, 1999), "*Guardian* Saturday Pages," p. 6.

20. Nicholas Lezard, "Believe in Evil," *The Guardian* (London), (January 8, 2000), "*Guardian* Saturday Pages," p. 11.

21. It is most unusual for a novelist's work to so consistently win awards. Even *The Bean Trees* appeared on final lists for prestigious awards, and *Animal Dreams* won the PEN/USA West Fiction Award and the Edward Abbey Award for Ecofiction. It was also an ABBY finalist, an American Library Association Notable Book, and a *New York Times* Notable Book. With *Pigs in Heaven*, Kingsolver repeated inclusion in these lists and also won the *Los Angeles Times* Fiction Prize, the Mountains and Plains Booksellers Award for Fiction, and the Cowboy Hall of Fame Western Fiction Award.

22. Hillary Clinton, "Bookshelf," *O, The Oprah Magazine* (July-August, 2000), p. 224.

4. The Novel's Performance

1. Jennifer Schuessler, "Men, Women and Coyotes," *New York Times Book Review* (November 5, 2000).

2. Ibid.

3. Barbara Kingsolver, "Dialogue" section, Barbara Kingsolver website.

4. Ibid.

5. Ibid.

6. Barbara Kingsolver, *The Poisonwood Bible*, p. 540.

7. Barbara Kingsolver, "Dialogue" section, Kingsolver website.

8. "Barbara Kingsolver" film.

9. Barbara Kingsolver, "Dialogue" section, Kingsolver website; see her review, "Survival of the Fittest," *New York Times Book Review* (Oct. 11, 1998), pp. 13–14.

10. Kingsolver interview, November 24, 1995, transcript. In the film, she states it even more bluntly: "If you're poor, you feel as if you've done something wrong."

11. Ibid.

12. Kingsolver, *The Poisonwood Bible*, p. 488.

13. Barbara Kingsolver, "Dialogue" section, Kingsolver website.

5. Further Reading and Discussion Questions

1. Meredith Sue Willis, "Barbara Kingsolver, Moving On," *Appalachian Journal* 22, no. 1 (Fall 1994), pp. 78–86; this, p. 80.

2. Maureen Ryan, "Barbara Kingsolver's Lowfat Fiction," *Journal of American Culture* 18, no. 4 (Winter 1995), pp. 77–82; this, p. 77.

3. Roberta Rubenstein, "*Homeric* Resonances: Longing and Belonging in Barbara Kingsolver's *Animal Dreams*," *Homemaking: Women Writers and the Politics and Poetics of Home*, ed. Catherine Wiley and Fiona Barnes. New York: Garland, 1996, pp. 5–22; this, p. 5.

4. Charlotte M. Wright, "Barbara Kingsolver" in *Updating the Literary West*, ed. Max Westbrook and Dan Flores. Ft. Worth, Texas: Texas Christian University Press, 1997, pp. 504–11; this, p. 510.

5. Ibid.

6. Barbara Kingsolver, "Dialogue" segments, Barbara Kingsolver website, 2001.

Bibliography

Books

The Bean Trees. New York: HarperCollins, 1988.
Homeland and Other Stories. New York: HarperCollins, 1989.
Holding the Line: Women in the Great Arizona Mine Strike of 1983. Ithaca, New York: ILR/Cornell University Press, 1989.
Animal Dreams. New York: HarperCollins, 1990.
Another America/Otra America. Spanish translations by Rebeca Cartes. Seattle, WA: The Seal Press, 1992.
High Tide in Tucson, Essays from Now or Never. New York: HarperCollins, 1992.
Pigs in Heaven. New York: HarperCollins, 1993.
The Poisonwood Bible. New York: HarperCollins, 1998.
Prodigal Summer. New York: HarperCollins, 2000.

Essays and Reviews (select)

"Albert Uplifts Anything" (review of Clyde Edgerton's *The Floatplane Notebooks*), *New York Times Book Review* (October 8, 1989), p. 10.
"Some Can Whistle" [by Larry McMurtry], *New York Times Book Review* (October 22, 1989, p. 8.

"Notes from Underground" (review of Priscilla Long's *Where the Sun Never Shines*), *Women's Review of Books*, 7, no. 9 (June, 1990), pp. 21–22.

"River of Traps: A Village Life" [by William deBuys and Alex Harris], *New York Times Book Review* (September 23, 1990), pp. 33, 50.

"Worlds in Collision" (review of Linda Hogan's *Mean Spirit*), *Los Angeles Times Book Review* (November 4, 1990), p. 3.

"Fish Fall From the Sky for a Reason: The Stories of Eva Luna" [by Isabel Allende], trans. Margaret Sayers Peden. *New York Times Book Review* (January 20, 1991), pp. 13–14.

"Whipsawed in Washington" (review of Annie Dillard's *The Living*), *The Nation*, 254, no. 20 (May 25, 1992), pp. 692–94.

"Where Love Is Nurtured and Confined: A Review of *Me and My Baby View the Eclipse* by Lee Smith," *Friendship and Sympathy: Communities of Southern Women Writers*, ed. Rosemary M. Magee. Jackson: University Press of Mississippi, 1992, pp. 255–57.

"Interview," *Backtalk: Women Writers Speak Out*, ed. Donna Perry. New Brunswick, NJ: Rutgers University Press, 1993, pp. 143–69.

"Desert Heat: *So Far From God* by Ana Castillo," *Los Angeles Times Book Review* (May 16, 1993), pp. 1, 9.

"*Brazil*" [by John Updike], *New York Times Book Review* (February 6, 1994), pp. 1, 26–27.

"A Metaphysics of Resistance" (review of Maria Elena Lucas's *Forged Under the Sun*), *Women's Review of Books*, 11, no. 5 (February, 1994), pp. 25–26.

"Not in Their Backyard" (review of A. G. Mojtabal's *Called Out*), *New York Times Book Review* (June 19, 1994), p. 4.

"Downscale in Topanga Canyon" (review of T. Coraghessan Boyle's *The Tortilla Curtain*), *The Nation*, 261, no. 9 (September 25, 1995), pp. 326–27.

"Barbara Kingsolver, Dear Mom," *I've Always Meant to Tell You: Letters to Our Mothers/An Anthology of Contemporary Women Writers*, ed. Constance Warloe. New York: Pocket Books, 1997, pp. 248–61.

"Making Peace," *Intimate Nature: the Bond Between Women and Animals*, ed. Linda Hogan et al. New York: Ballantine, 1998, pp. 250–57.

"Survival of the Fittest" (review of Cathleen Schine's *The Evolution of Jane*), *New York Times Book Review* (October 11, 1998), pp. 13–14.

"Deadline," *A Map of Hope: Women's Writings on Human Rights, An International Literary Anthology*, ed. Marjorie Agosin. New Brunswick, NJ: Rutgers University Press, 1999, pp. 70–71.

"How Poems Happen," *The Beacon Best of 1999: Creative Writing by Women and Men of All Colors*, ed. N. Shange. Boston: Beacon, 1999, pp. 252–54.